"Anita Posch is one of the most productive and insightful German voices in the Bitcoin space. Her work makes Bitcoin approachable, understandable and compelling to those who are new to Bitcoin and helps them on their journey to become experts. In an environment filled with noise, her work is crystal clear and honest." – ANDREAS M. ANTONOPOULOS, AUTHOR "MASTERING BITCOIN" AND "THE INTERNET OF MONEY"

"Anita has done tremendous work in the Bitcoin community, including and especially the content she has produced about Bitcoin's use in less-privileged regions of the world. Her book is a concise and approachable introduction to Bitcoin that covers all of the major topics for someone to get started." – LYN ALDEN, INVESTMENT STRATEGIST

"'What is Bitcoin?' To even begin to start answering this question, one must first ask 'what is money?' Anita takes the reader through this journey of learning about money so that they can understand why Bitcoin is the next leap forward in financial technology. Once you know the 'why?' then there is the issue of 'how?' With great sovereignty comes great responsibility; in order to safely navigate this new system you'll need the knowledge and tools that this book provides." – JAMESON LOPP, CO-FOUNDER & CTO, CASA

"Anita is one of the preeminent Bitcoin educators, demonstrating an unmatched breadth of interest and curiosity. Her book is a fitting summary to her tireless work, and represents an invaluable contribution to the ever-growing and rich body of knowledge surrounding Bitcoin." – NIC CARTER, PARTNER, CASTLE ISLAND VENTURES

"Anita has distilled what has taken most Bitcoiners years to learn (myself included) into a few hour read. The masterful organization and flow from one subject area to the next actually make Bitcoin seem simple to explain. It is hard to believe she is able to tackle the enormity of Bitcoin in so few pages. Anita handily dispels the ill-informed criticism in the west that Bitcoin is a solution in search of a problem. She gives numerous clear and understandable examples of how Bitcoin improves the lives of those who have been excluded and/or enslaved by the current financial system. This book is a must read for government officials and non-profits who want to really understand why projects like Bitcoin Beach can bring economic empowerment instead of the economic dependence that often results from fiat-based development efforts." – MICHAEL PETERSON, BITCOIN BEACH, EL SALVADOR

"The best teachers are students. Since the first day that Anita popped up on my radar, she has been a curious and insightful researcher and promoter of Bitcoin's revolutionary technology. Gleaning wheat from chaff, she writes with the simplicity, clarity, and precision necessary for a complex topic demanding expertise in multiple disciplines. Sovryn is proud to sponsor the publication of (L)earn Bitcoin as part of our mission to make Bitcoin unstoppable." – EXILEDSURFER, FOUNDER, PARALLELE POLIS, COMMS LEAD AT SOVRYNBTC

"It is no simple task to explain Bitcoin, the new elephant in the room of finance. Like blind men, specialists often limit their description to a narrow field of expertise. Anita's angle of attack is holistic, synthetic and clear. It brings a fresh look to 'the people's money'." – THOMAS VOEGTLIN, FOUNDER & CEO, ELECTRUM

"It has been great to see Anita's journey over the past several years, speaking to and learning from the best in the industry, all around the world, and making it accessible to beginners. One of the hardest workers in the space, and a great person to learn from!" – HASS MCCOOK, ENGINEER AND BITCOIN EVANGELIST

"Anita Posch is one of the inspiring voices in the Bitcoin sphere. Her inclusive approach and engaging writing style will offer an easy start for a novice as well as experienced Bitcoiners and crypto-folks. Great reading for anyone interested in all things crypto." – JUKKA BLOMBERG, CHIEF MARKETING OFFICER, LOCALBITCOINS

"Buying bitcoin is easier than ever today. Storing your own bitcoin long-term and safely requires a minimum of technical and economic understanding. This book provides the necessary basics to keep you in control of your money. Wherever the Bitcoin journey takes us, investing in this book is a sure win." – JOHANNES GRILL, PRESIDENT BITCOIN AUSTRIA

(L)EARN BITCOIN

BECOME FINANCIALLY SOVRYN

ANITA POSCH

(L)earn Bitcoin
Become Financially Sovryn
1st Edition, June 2021

Author: Anita Posch

Publisher: PoshMedia e.U., Seilerstaette 24, 4. Stock, 1010 Wien

Editor: Mark Kersley
Typesetting: Couper Street Type Co.
Cover Design/Art Direction: tzu jan | 自然
Illustration Concept Sketch: @danubastidas
Illustration: Maleek Illustration
Hand Lettering: Mila Masina

ISBN (hb): 978-3-9504591-6-6
ISBN (pb): 978-3-9504591-5-9
ISBN (ebook): 978-3-9504591-4-2

Get current information about the book online at https://learnbitcoin.link

"The root problem with conventional currency is all the trust that's required to make it work. The central bank must be trusted not to debase the currency, but the history of fiat currencies is full of breaches of that trust."

SATOSHI NAKAMOTO

June 9, 2021
A few hours ago I was live on Twitter Spaces together with 20,000 Bitcoiners and the President of El Salvador when the country's congress voted to adopt bitcoin as legal tender, making it the world's first country to do so. Coincidentally I am also finishing the manuscript of this book today. What an incredible time to be alive and I'm humbled to be able to contribute to this movement through my Bitcoin education. By picking up this book and sharing it with your friends we are hastening the monetary revolution towards more individual freedom and sovereignty.

ANITA POSCH

Contents

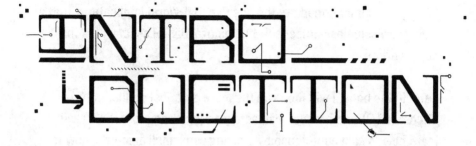

INTRODUCTION

"Writing a description for this thing for general audiences is bloody hard. There's nothing to relate it to." – SATOSHI NAKAMOTO

(L)earn Bitcoin is the best guide to decide why and how you should enter the world of Bitcoin. It presents Bitcoin in all its facets, from its technical, economical, political and social implications to how it is evolving in the current monetary landscape. It provides a step-by-step roadmap to navigate this new financial world and sets you up with concrete recommendations on how to safely acquire, earn and store bitcoin. Ascending the staircase of financial sovereignty will grant you personal freedom and control over your money.

In this book you will find answers to the questions of what money is, where it comes from, its historical development, blockchain technology and Bitcoin specifically. It gives answers to the questions of why and how to use Bitcoin, while debunking popular myths and misunderstandings surrounding cryptocurrencies. I take a deep dive into Bitcoin's development since its inception in 2008 and give an outlook on future applications of money based on Bitcoin.

While mainstream media and economic pundits in the Western world think that it's just a tool for speculation, my goal is to spread the word about Bitcoin as an enabler of financial fairness and social change. What goes unmentioned are the positive real-world implications that a truly permissionless, uncensorable, neutral digital asset with a fixed supply offers.

Later in the book, I will focus on the more practical applications of bitcoin (BTC) and how you can safely acquire and store it. You will learn how to gain confidence by starting with small amounts, how to minimize the existing risks and proceed strategically and efficiently in storing your wealth for the long-term.

This is neither financial advice nor a trading guide to the thousands of Altcoins in existence. If you are only interested in short-term gains, treating money like you're gambling in a casino, this book is not for you. It's for people who want to (l)earn and understand the fundamentals of Bitcoin and control their funds in a self-sovereign manner.

THE EVOLUTION OF MONEY

On January 3, 2009, Bitcoin was born. Since its creation, the Bitcoin P2P network Internet Protocol (IP) has attached new blocks of data to a chain of transactions approximately every 10 minutes. The Bitcoin blockchain stores transactions in the correct chronological order which cannot be altered afterwards, as fixed as time itself. Just as our heartbeat preserves our bodies, this process is preserved by a system that draws its foundations from cryptography, game theory, IT, and decentralized networks that keep itself in balance.

This self-regulating system has the following characteristics:

- Bitcoin transactions are censorship resistant.
- Bitcoin is immutable.
- Bitcoin cannot be counterfeited.
- Bitcoin transactions are highly secure without intermediaries, like a bank.
- Bitcoin transactions are transparent, publicly visible and can be audited by anybody.

PayPal payment vs. Bitcoin

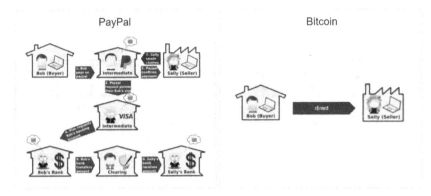

A PayPal payment vs. Bitcoin

Source: Illustration NetGuardians retrieved April 2017, https://www.netguardians.ch/ngfintechblog/2016/11/17/blockchain-explained-part-1

In a traditional payment there are up to seven intermediaries until the payment reaches the recipient. Bitcoin has none.

- Bitcoin is a neutral network: it does not moralize or distinguish between "good" and "bad" payments.
- Bitcoin is permissionless: there are no gatekeepers that can prevent its use.
- Bitcoin is borderless: it can be used worldwide.
- Bitcoin, the Internet Protocol, is a common good: it belongs to everybody, not a single entity such as a company.
- The rules of Bitcoin are enforced by the programmatically secure consensus of all parties involved.

Bitcoin is people's money. Bitcoin is the evolution of money. It is a continuation of the perpetual process of discovering new money that has always been a part of the history of mankind. Over the millennia, various new forms of money have been found and used, from a direct exchange between people to a credit system in a gold standard, to fiat currency to today's current non-backed inflationary system. The banking and monetary system as we know it today has existed and evolved for about 300 years. It is only natural that, with the emergence of a new form of communication via the internet, a new form of economy and a new type of money, namely internet-native money, should arise.

From metals to Bitcoin

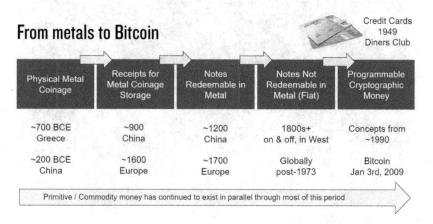

Physical Metal Coinage	Receipts for Metal Coinage Storage	Notes Redeemable in Metal	Notes Not Redeemable in Metal (Fiat)	Programmable Cryptographic Money
~700 BCE Greece	~900 China	~1200 China	1800s+ on & off, in West	Concepts from ~1990
~200 BCE China	~1600 Europe	~1700 Europe	Globally post-1973	Bitcoin Jan 3rd, 2009

Credit Cards 1949 Diners Club

Primitive / Commodity money has continued to exist in parallel through most of this period

History of money

Source: Anita Posch, Credits: University of Nicosia, MOOC in Digital Currency, "A brief history of money" with image: Lotus Head, CC BY-SA 3.0, wikimedia.org

Programmable cryptographic money or the "Internet of Money" – as Andreas M. Antonopoulos puts it – is unstoppable. We are at the beginning of a new era in the history of mankind.

1.1 Rai Stones of Yap

If Bitcoin sounds mind-boggling and you can't grasp the concept of a blockchain as a shared ledger of truth, the Rai of the Isle of Yap is a good example to introduce some overlapping concepts.

Rai are large stone disks used on Yap island in the Western Pacific (Micronesia). They were "minted" from the limestone deposits of the island of Palau and used as a currency until the 20th century.

STONE MONEY OF UAP, WESTERN CAROLINE ISLANDS.
(From the paper by Dr. W. H. Furness, 3rd, in Transactions, Department of Archæology, University of Pennsylvania, Vol. I., No. 1, p. 51, Fig. 3, 1904.)

Rai stones with carrying logs, 1903
Source: Image: "Stone Money of Uap, Western Caroline Islands." – Dr. Caroline Furness Jayne took this photograph during a 1903 stay on Yap, Public domain, via Wikimedia Commons

Rai stones were brought to Yap via boat and, due to their size and weight, were not moved when spent, but simply changed owners. Every transaction was "recorded" orally within the small community, with the stone's ownership history becoming common knowledge. Eventually, the transaction "history"/"ledger" became the only part that mattered. A stone was once dropped by the canoe transferring it to Yap and sank. The stone was deemed to still be money, since it still existed, even though no one has seen or had access to it since.

This is particularly important because it demonstrates a naturally occurring use of a ledger of transactions. The ledger was shared orally between the inhabitants and attributed ownership and delegated property without a single stone moving; everyone agreed on it and a consensus was formed. This is how we can make a comparison to the functions of the Bitcoin blockchain; it is a shared ledger of all transactions, stored simultaneously on thousands of computers (nodes) globally.[2]

Another similarity to Bitcoin is the actually creation of Rai stone, which was work intense and a form of proof-of-work. The stones were carved out with hand tools, quarried overseas and brought to the island via canoe. Once the Rai stones became easy to manufacture with modern techniques, they became less useful as money, because they were no longer a reliable indicator of energy spent.

Rai stones have been viewed by modern economists as a primitive form of money, and are often used as an example to support the thesis that the value of some forms of money can be assigned purely through a shared belief in said value.[3] Today's money is not backed by anything either. In fact, it is only established and declared legal tender by government regulation. Because of this, it is the medium of account we use and is therefore perceived as valuable.

1.2 How Money Is Created

"The central bank must be trusted not to debase the currency, but the history of fiat currencies is full of breaches of that trust." – SATOSHI NAKAMOTO

Learning about Bitcoin was an eye-opener for me. There are two distinct periods of my life, one before Bitcoin and one after Bitcoin.

---

2 Wikipedia Rai stones, https://en.wikipedia.org/wiki/Rai_stones
3 University of Nicosia, Introduction to Digital Currencies, Session I, p. 15

I see things completely differently today. In my goal to understand Bitcoin, I first had to understand the current monetary system. What are the differences between currency systems like the USD or Euro and Bitcoin? What is inflation? What role are central banks playing, and so on? It's puzzling that we do not learn these concepts in school, but this specific lack of education may, unfortunately, be intentional.

180 currencies are used in 195 countries around the world. A currency is a system of money in common use, defined by governments. Many jurisdictions define their national currency as legal tender; it is money declared by law to be valid for the payment of debts that cannot be refused as a method of payment.

All 180 currencies – the US Dollar, the Euro, the Yen and the Pound Sterling, for example – can be defined as being within a category called 'fiat money'. Since 1971, none of these fiat currencies has been backed by gold or by any other tangible asset. Money has value because we believe in it. Money is a language to express how valuable something is, socially. The word fiat stems from Latin and means "let it be done". Current money is created through an entry in a digital ledger and is just a number in an accounting system. There is no creation of real-world productivity behind it.

Who is in charge of the creation of money? It's a mix of governments and central banks, together with commercial banks. It's a centralized, hierarchical system with gatekeepers. There is no agreement on a supply limit or emission rate.

Fiat is "money by decree"; it's coercively managed through the state's implicit threat of violence. Value is being maintained by the creation of an endless tax liability that you can only satisfy with fiat money and by state-administered security markets, as well as legal tender laws and tax policy.

- Money is created by central banks in the form of paper money and coins.
- Central banks buy assets and bonds from the open market, money flows into the system.
- Money is created through government stimulus, through benefits, grants and bail outs.
- Money is created by commercial banks through loans.

1.2.1 Money Is Created Through Debt

The last point is one we all know. It is how we take out a loan to buy a house, start a business or buy a car. The process is easy, but only for those who are already privileged. If you cannot put forward some security as collateral, you are a small business owner, you do not have a regular fixed income job, or you are a woman in a country where women are still forbidden to own any property, then you will probably not qualify for credit at your bank. If you do get the loan, the bank edits its digital ledger and adds the credit sum to its account. You then owe them the loan amount plus the rate of interest. You must now go out and work or sell something in order to be able to pay back the loan plus the interest rate. It's a great deal for the banks. They add nothing, but earn the fees for your loan agreement and the interest on your payback.

On top of that, there is something called fractional-reserve banking. This allows banks to lend out more money than they hold in reserves or as balances in their account at the central bank. The minimum amount that banks must hold in liquid assets, called the "reserve ratio", is determined by the central bank. This rate varies from country to country. In the Euro area, banks have to hold a minimum of 1% at the time of writing. In March 2020 the FED abolished this minimum reserve requirement due to the

COVID-19 pandemic. Canada, the UK, New Zealand, Australia, Sweden and Hong Kong all have no reserve requirements. If each of us were to go to the bank today and request to withdraw our money, the banking system would fall apart. Because the banks have lent out more money than they own, they would be unable to give you back your own money.

In 2020 global debt rose by an incredible 24 trillion to 281 trillion USD, or 355% of global GDP.[4]

1.2.2 Central Banks as Lenders of Last Resort

Commercial banks can and have called for the help of the central bank as lenders of last resort. In 2008/2009 the banks, who were responsible for the global financial crisis, received their bail-out money. They were rescued because they were "too big to fail". And what did they do with the money? They bought back shares in their own companies. Nothing "trickled down" into the economy. The gap between rich and poor inevitably became bigger and bigger.

Central banks are called lenders of last resort. The objective is to prevent economic disruption as a result of financial panics, and bank runs spreading from one bank to the next due to a lack of liquidity. Financial actors like banks know that the central banks will have to bail them out, which leads to moral hazard – excessive risk-taking by both bankers and investors.

The creation of artificial money through central banks overshadowed the distortion in the market. Because of the flooding and manipulation of the monetary system with cheap money, there is no rational price

---

4 Debt to GDP ratio

Sharp surge in debt-to-GDP ratios

percentage points, estimated change in debt ratios in 2020

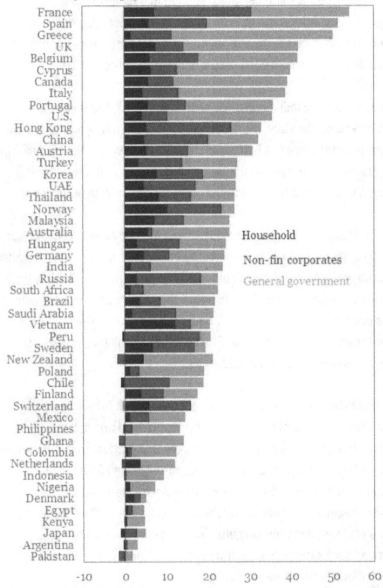

Legend:
- Household
- Non-fin corporates
- General government

Source: IIF, BIS, IMF, National sources

Debt to GDP ratio

Source: Debt to GDP ratio, JS Blokland, https://twitter.com/jsblokland/status/1362138620665221122?s=20

finding mechanism anymore. Usually, supply and demand determine
the value of goods and commodities but, in a distorted and
manipulated market, there is no room for fair price discovery. The
global middle class is paying for the financial elites' greed which, in
turn, is being fed by a corrupted system of money creation.

Have you, as an individual, ever been bailed out? And if you have,
would you do the same thing over and over again, rigging the system
knowing that there is a last resort, which will always bail you out? This
is exactly what banks, Wall Street, Hedge Funds and their lobbying
lawyers do constantly, assisted by central banks all over the world.

"Classically, central banks hold reserves in case of emergencies, set
interest rates, and allocate funds to stimulate or slow economies after
disruptive events like panics or wars. The more recent role they have
assumed is one of securing the entire financial system and influencing
the economic trajectory of entire sovereign nations. This is the
antithesis of democratic rule. Such a monetary oligarchy operates
beyond democratic norms and limits."[5]

Naomi Prins' book tapped into the psyche of Wall Street, revealing how
the very structure of the financial system hinged on traders flocking to
the next big bet, regardless of the stakes. In addition, the *same* people
and families kept popping up, cycling through Wall Street and
Washington. They influenced the economy beneath them from their
loftier heights of status, private money and public office, dismantling
laws that stood in their way and finding loopholes through others.
Private banks normalized market manipulation. Central banks made it
an art form, with no limits."[6]

---

5 Collusion, by Nomi Prins, Bold Type Books, 2019, p. 7
6 Collusion, by Nomi Prins, Bold Type Books, 2019, p. xvii

1.2.3 Money Supply Inflation

Let's take the US Dollar as an example for all fiat currencies. Because of money supply inflation, the more USD that are available, the less value a single note has. Imagine a banknote as a commodity like copper. If there is more copper on the market than there is demand, the price of copper is falling; its value is decreasing. The same is true for your banknote. The value of fiat currencies is determined by supply and demand too. If you increase the supply and the demand stays the same, the value of one unit decreases.

The money supply consists of various types of money that are generally classified as Ms, such as M0 (base money), M1, M2 and M3. The definitions might vary slightly in different countries.

The monetary base (M0) is the total amount of a currency in physical paper and coin that is either in circulation in the hands of the public or in the form of commercial bank deposits held in the central bank's reserves.[7]

As long as you hold cash, it is an asset like bitcoin, a property that you own. If you take your cash and store it at the bank, you have a claim, but don't own the money anymore. Similar to bitcoin at an exchange.

Any other fiat money supply (M1, M2, M3) is comprised of claims on base money.[8]

M1 includes M0, demand deposits, traveler's checks, and other checkable deposits, that are easily convertible to cash.

---

7 Monetary Base, https://www.investopedia.com/terms/m/monetarybase.asp
8 Global Monetary Base, Crypto Voices, https://cryptovoices.com/basemoney

M2 includes M0, M1, money market securities, mutual funds and other time deposits. These assets are less liquid than M1 and not as suitable as exchange mediums, but they can be quickly converted into cash or checking deposits. M2 is closely watched as an indicator of money supply and future inflation, and as a target for central bank monetary policy.

The amount of M2 currency in circulation in the US was **19.7 trillion USD** in February 2021.[9] Look at the growth in 2020.

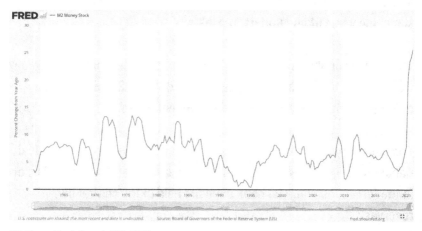

M2 Money Stock Growth USA, 2021
Source: FRED, M2 Money Stock, https://fred.stlouisfed.org/series/M2SL

"We accept this as normal because we assume it will never end. The fractional reserve banking system has functioned around the world for hundreds of years (first gold-backed, and then totally fiat-based), albeit with occasional inflationary events along the way to partially reset things.

Each individual unit of fiat currency has degraded about 99% in value or more over a multi-decade timeline. This means that investors either need to earn a rate of interest that exceeds the real inflation rate (which is not

---

9 FRED, M2 Money Stock, https://fred.stlouisfed.org/series/M2SL

currently happening), or they need to buy investments instead, which inflates the value of stocks and real estate compared to their cash flows and pushes up the prices of scarce objects like fine art."[10]

Adding to money supply inflation is the fact that the population in the US and other western nations is not growing at the same rate as the money supply. "US population used to grow at maybe 1.5% per year, and now grows closer to 0.5% per year. That's pretty important. Meanwhile, broad money supply is up 25% year over year, and is on track to be up 75%+ over a rolling 5-year period in the future."[11]

Strictly speaking, inflation occurs when the money supply outstrips nominal GDP growth, which consists of population and productivity growth. The Consumer Price Index of the USA shows that the prices for goods went up since the value of money has declined.

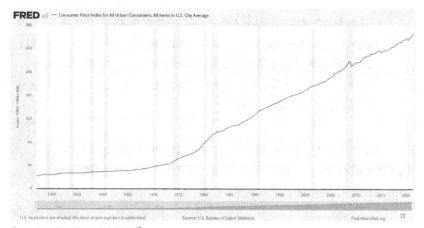

Consumer Price Index US 2020[12]
Source: US Consumer Price Index, https://fred.stlouisfed.org/series/CPIAUCSL

---

10 Lyn Alden, Ponzi scheme, https://www.lynalden.com/bitcoin-ponzi-scheme/
11 Lyn Alden, https://twitter.com/LynAldenContact/status/1362912907659522049?s=20
12 US Consumer Price Index, https://fred.stlouisfed.org/series/CPIAUCSL

1.2.4 Ponzi Scheme

> Ponzi scheme: "A form of fraud in which belief in the success of a fictive enterprise is fostered by payment of quick returns to first investors from money invested by others." – OXFORD ENGLISH DICTIONARY

Bitcoin enemies call it a Ponzi scheme. I say, they either do not understand Bitcoin or what the real Ponzi system is, or they have a vested interest in Bitcoin not succeeding. Charles Ponzi was arrested in the US in 1920 for taking $20 million dollars from tens of thousands of victims. His promise was to double their money within three months. In return for cash, investors received promissory notes that guaranteed the original investment plus 50 percent interest. These notes bore Ponzi's ink-stamped signature. Many referred to them as "Ponzi notes".

> "My business was simple. It was the old game of robbing Peter to pay Paul. You would give me one hundred dollars and I would give you a note to pay you one-hundred-and-fifty dollars in three months...My notes became more valuable than American money...Then came trouble. The whole thing was broken." – CHARLES PONZI

If you want to know more, listen to my podcast episode about the life and story of Italian-born Charles Ponzi. You can find it at https://anita.link/ponzi.

Characteristics of a Ponzi Scheme

- A Ponzi scheme has a centralized actor, leader or organization that collects investments and runs off in the end.
- Ponzi schemes are not auditable or transparent. Nobody except the creator knows what happens to the funds.

- A Ponzi scheme issues money until it breaks – there is no supply limit.
- Difficulty in repaying investors: the more money that flows into the scheme, the more money has to be paid back, and the more difficult it gets for the creator to stop the machine.
- The system has to break one day – there is no way out.
- The scammers earn money for lending out funds with no real contribution to the economic performance of a country.
- Greed is driving the Ponzi scheme. Retail investors who get in early, earn interest and tell others, who also want to get rich quick.

Let's compare these characteristics to today's system of money creation.

Characteristics of Fiat Money Creation

- Centralized actors like governments, central banks and commercial banks create money.
- The monetary system is not auditable or transparent.
- There is no money supply limit.
- Difficulty in repaying investors: due to the fractional-reserve banking system, if only 20% of a bank's customers where to request a payout at the same time the bank gets into trouble and will say "no" to your withdrawal. This happens regularly around the world and happened to some US banks in early 2020 during the pandemic shutdown.
- The system has to break one day – there is no way out.
- Banks earn money for lending out funds with no real contribution to the economic performance of a country.
- Greed is driving the fiat system. Financial elites receive cheap loans because they own securities to buy more securities and grow their wealth and power.

1.2.5 The Real Ponzi Scheme

- The only similarity between Bitcoin and a Ponzi scheme is the network effect of greed. But unlike a Ponzi, you can hold the keys to your bitcoin yourself. There is no bank or centralized actor controlling your bitcoin.
- Bitcoin has a limited supply. Only 21 million will ever be created. Bitcoin is finite, fiat currency is infinite. There can be no money supply based inflation in Bitcoin.
- Bitcoin's issuance is predetermined by an algorithm that all actors in Bitcoin have agreed upon and secure via operating nodes. It can not be altered without the consent of the global Bitcoin community. Since the 21 million bitcoin limit is one of the most important features of Bitcoin, an agreement for changing it will be very hard or even impossible to achieve.
- Central bankers are determining the financial fate of all countries around the world. They are not elected, but they act as governments trying to control the entire financial market.
- The Cantillon effect was described by Irish-French economist Richard Cantillon around 1730. He suggested that inflation occurs gradually and that the new supply of money created by the banks has a localised effect on inflation, rewarding the bankers and close actors by artificially creating money, benefiting those closest to the origin of money.

"The Fed's crisis and post-crisis monetary policies, adopted by other major central banks, was supposed to "trickle down" to the masses. That didn't happen. The global elites knew this then, and they are more aware of it now. In January 2017, the World Economic Forum admitted that rising inequality threatens the world economy. These colluders provoke inequality because it benefits them and the preservation of their global power hierarchies to the detriment of everything and everyone else." – NOMI PRINS[13]

1.2.6 The End of This Kind of Growth

Wealth inequality has been rising in the last few centuries, along with the commodification and monetization of natural resources. Nothing is left to be consumed. We are living through a fight for resources, for equal opportunities against the establishment and elites enriching themselves through corruption and financial advantages.

"Another by-product of the financial crisis and central bank collusion was the rise in economic anxiety that spawned a swing towards nationalism, from Brazil to Great Britain to the United States. The shock of Brexit in the United Kingdom reverberated around the world as voters turned away from the incumbent leadership and its failed economic policies. In the United States, the election victory of Donald Trump, the billionaire 'antiestablishment' president, was another manifestation of this trend. These landmark votes were not caused by central banking policy directly but were the effects."[14]

The growing divide between rich and poor is based on our current monetary system, which is the real Ponzi scheme. Central bankers are not democratically elected, yet they decide the financial fate of the world. Bankers and their friends are profiting from this system. It is time for an alternative: a decentralized, open, neutral, transparent, immutable, non-inflatable and collaborative form of money for the people: Bitcoin.

---

13 Collusion, by Nomi Prins, Bold Type Books, 2019, p. 253
14 Collusion, by Nomi Prins, Bold Type Books, 2019, p. 249

1.2.7 Today's Petrodollar System

Now that we have discussed how money is created, let's dive into the world of currency wars and how this system of national currencies is exclusive and has, historically, been dominated by different empires.

The history of currency wars is long. "Over the past century the world went from a gold standard system, to the Bretton Woods system, to the Petrodollar system. Each system mostly unraveled from within rather than being brought down externally, and each time one system transitioned to another, a significant and widespread currency devaluation occurred."[15]

The British monetary hegemony lasted from 1871 to World War I. Back then a nation's currency was pegged to gold. After the interwar period, when monetary power began to decentralize, the United States emerged as the central money powerhouse after the allied victory in the Second World War. The Bretton Woods system, founded in 1944, was the first example of a fully negotiated monetary order, intended to govern monetary relations among independent states. It set a system of rules, institutions, and procedures to regulate the international monetary system, like the International Monetary Fund (IMF). The United States, which controlled two-thirds of the world's gold, insisted that the Bretton Woods system rests on both gold and the US dollar. Soviet representatives attended the conference but later declined to ratify the final agreements, insisting that the institutions they had created were "branches of Wall Street". This can be interpreted as the starting point of the Cold War.

---

15 Lyn Alden, The Structure of the Global Monetary System, https://www.lynalden.com/fraying-petrodollar-system/

On 15 August 1971, the United States, lead by President Richard Nixon, unilaterally terminated the convertibility of the US dollar to gold, effectively bringing the Bretton Woods system to an end and rendering the dollar a fiat currency. At the same time, many fixed currencies (such as the pound sterling) also became free-floating.

Today's monetary system is built on the Petrodollar. Lyn Alden describes this in her article "The Structure of the Global Monetary System":

"Beginning in 1971 after the breakdown of the Bretton Woods system, currencies around the world all became fiat currencies, and the global monetary system became less ordered. This was the first time in human history that this happened, where all currencies in the world at the same time were rendered into unbacked paper.

Fiat currency is a monetary system whereby there is nothing of value in the currency itself; it's just paper, cheap metal coins, or digital bits of information. It has value because the government declares it to have value and that it is legal tender to pay all things including taxes.

A country can enforce the usage of a fiat currency as a medium of exchange and unit of account within their country by making all taxes payable only in that currency, or by enacting other laws to add friction to, or in some cases outright ban, other mediums of exchange and units of account. If their currency has a big enough problem, though, as is the case for many emerging markets, a black market will develop for other mediums of exchange, such as foreign currency or hard assets.

A fiat currency can face particular problems when trying to be used outside of its home country. Why should businesses and governments

in other countries accept pieces of paper, which can be printed endlessly by a foreign government and have no firm backing, as a form of payment for their valuable goods and services? Without a real backing, what is it worth? Why would you sell oil to foreigners for paper?

In the early 1970's, there were a variety of geopolitical conflicts including the Yom Kippur War and the OPEC oil embargo. In 1974, however, the United States and Saudi Arabia reached an agreement, and from there, the world was set on the petrodollar system; a clever way to make a global fiat currency system work decently enough.... With the petrodollar system, Saudi Arabia (and other countries in OPEC) sell their oil exclusively in dollars in exchange for US protection and cooperation. Even if France wants to buy oil from Saudi Arabia, for example, they do so in dollars....In return, the United States uses its unrivaled blue-water navy to protect global shipping lanes, and preserve the geopolitical status quo with military action or the threat thereof as needed....Some of us, particularly near the top of the income ladder, directly or indirectly benefit from this system. Americans who work around finance, government, healthcare, and technology get many of the benefits of living in the hegemonic power, without the drawbacks. On the other hand, Americans who make physical products tend not to benefit, because they lost their jobs or had their incomes suppressed, and thus haven't benefited from the gains. And outside of the United States, exporting countries benefit from the system, while countries that don't like how the global monetary system is structured don't have much recourse to do anything about it, unless they get big enough like Russia and China."[16]

---

16 Lyn Alden, Petrodollar System (1974-Present), https://www.lynalden.com/fraying-petrodollar-system/

We have been in currency wars for many decades. Which currency is stronger? Which country can gain more benefits from manipulating its currency? The Euro, the US Dollar, the Chinese Yuan? Or even Facebook's Diem? Corporation money is the new, strong player on the market. To retain their powers central banks started to work on their own digital currencies (CBDCs).

New forms of money emerge
Source: Anita Posch

Bitcoin is our alternative to this system. Protecting our privacy in this digital age, voting against the abuse of monopolistic power in the current system, and giving people living in authoritarian states with corrupt rulers the same opportunities to participate in the economic system. Bitcoin is a defence strategy, a tool with which we can preserve the human right to transactional freedom and privacy.

1.3 Bitcoin – Money for the Digital Age

If people ask what Bitcoin is, my first and shortest answer is: Bitcoin is digital cash. It's like the banknotes and coins in your pocket. It belongs to you, nobody can hinder you from spending it. If you use cash to buy a bicycle, you hand the seller your banknotes and coins. You do not need to trust the seller, because you got your bicycle and the shop got its money. The deal is closed without a bank, identification or credit card.

The same is true for bitcoin. When you buy something, whether on the Internet or in a store and pay with bitcoin, the value you are sending moves directly from you to the other person. Without a bank, without PayPal and without credit cards, the transaction remains secure, trustless and unforgeable – this is revolutionary.

The Bitcoin network is open source software and belongs to no one. It's a common good. There is no company behind Bitcoin. Anyone can download, run and view the code, and make suggestions for improvement without asking for permission. Any decision as to whether and how to make changes to the rules must be made by the consensus of all parties involved. There is no hierarchy. Bitcoin creates trust through merging techniques from different fields of science: cryptography, a globally distributed computer network, an unchangeable database of all transactions (blockchain) and a game-theoretical incentive system for securing the network and issuing the money (mining).

In contrast to fiat money like the Euro or USD, which are controlled by their respective central banks, this is a completely new system. Trust is not dependent on a hierarchical, political system but is built on mathematics, cryptography, and a self-regulating consensus system.

Bitcoin is built on a set of rules. It is a self-regulating system, based on mathematics and cryptography that is enforcing the issuance of newly minted coins on the basis of a protocol without arbitrary human interventions. Censorship of transactions or negative interest rates are not possible, therefore it is a reliable way of securing value and assets.

1.4 The History of Bitcoin

"The 2007-2008 US financial crisis was the consequence of a loosely regulated banking system in which power was concentrated in the hands of too limited a cast of speculators."[17]

"The 2007-2008 financial crisis that ravaged the global economy was ignited by a rapacious banking system in the United States. In response, herded by the Fed, the central banks of the G7 nations careened down an endless money-manufacturing trail – in broad day light."[18]

On October 31 2008, in the advent of the biggest financial crises the world has ever seen, someone going by the pseudonym Satoshi Nakamoto published a white paper called "Bitcoin: A Peer-to-Peer Electronic Cash System" on the domain bitcoin.org and proposed a new digital form of money.

On Jan 3 2009, the first public block of Bitcoin, the so-called Genesis Block, was mined. Satoshi left a message in it: "Chancellor on brink of second bailout for banks", which was the headline of the daily newspaper, The Times, in the UK on that same day. It's a timestamp that marks the beginning of Bitcoin and shows the intention that it should be an alternative to the current banking and financial system, in which you needed to trust intermediaries when you want to process electronic payments.

On June 9 2021, bitcoin became legal tender in El Salvador.

---

17 Collusion, by Nomi Prins, Bold Type Books, 2019, p. 1
18 Collusion, by Nomi Prins, Bold Type Books, 2019, p. 247

Since the 1990s, computer experts, mathematicians and cryptographers – including some women – have been working on concepts of creating digital money. Bitcoin could be created because it was built on the key technologies of its predecessors.

1.4.1 Cryptocurrency Projects Before Bitcoin

Parts of the following concepts were incorporated into Satoshi Nakamoto's Bitcoin white paper.

eCash DigiCash	Hashcash	B-Money	Bit Gold	Bitcoin
1990 David Chaum	1997 Cynthia Dwork & Moni Naor Adam Back	1998 Wei Dai	1997 / 1999 Nick Szabo	2008 Satoshi Nakamoto
Private and public keys	Proof-of-work	Distributed network	Decentralized issuance Smart Contracts	Adds blockchain Double-spending solved

Cryptocurrency projects before Bitcoin

Source: Anita Posch, Sources: The Merkle, https://themerkle.com/top-4-cryptocurrency-projects-created-ahead-of-bitcoin/, Hashcash.org, http://www.hashcash.org/bitcoin/

Public and Private Key Pairs

In 1990 David Chaum was concerned with the public nature and open access to online payments and personal information. He founded "Digicash", a corporation and electronic money of the same name, which used cryptographic protocols as well as private and public keys to anonymize transactions. The use of signatures – public and private key pairs – became essential in the further development of electronic money and Bitcoin.

Proof-of-Work

> The pyramids of Egypt are proof of work. They are a manifest of
> Egyptian culture, wealth and organization.

With the advent of the internet and email came the problem of
spam. To combat the growing problem of spam, in their 1992 paper
"Pricing via Processing or Combatting Junk Mail", Cynthia Dwork
and Moni Naor proposed the idea "...to require a user to compute a
moderately hard, but not intractable function..." before they are
technically able to send out emails. It meant that, if someone wants
to send a large number of emails at the same time, the computer
would need to solve a mathematical problem. This process takes
time and effort and kept the spammers from sending messages in
quick succession.

In 1997 Adam Back proposed a similar idea called "Hashcash". Satoshi
Nakamoto implemented Hashcash as the proof-of-work system used in
Bitcoin. Adam Back's work is cited in the Bitcoin white paper. Listen to
my interview with Adam Back from 2019 where we discuss his idea for
Hashcash and the evolution of his work up to Bitcoin. Find it at anita.
link/12

The term "proof-of-work" was first coined and formalized in a 1999
paper by Markus Jakobsson and Ari Juels.

Decentralization

Hashcash was followed by "B-Money" by Wei Dai in 1998. His concept
was the first to be based on a decentralized network of computers.
This is baked into Bitcoin's peer-to-peer network with computers
running the Bitcoin software as full nodes or miners. Peer-to-peer

means a system of equally privileged, equipotent participants without a hierarchy on the network.

A short time later, Nick Szabo published a paper on "BitGold", the first digital money system that was able to run without a central entity issuing the money. He is also the first person to present a paper on "Smart Contracts".

1.4.2 Solving the Double-Spending Problem

These predecessor money technologies had a major unresolved problem. The "double spending" problem means that already spent digital money could be used a second time. Imagine a PDF file that you can copy, modify and send endlessly at zero cost, claiming that each copy is the original. Such a digital file would be worthless as money.

Satoshi Nakamoto's ingenious idea was to add a ledger to the system with blocks that contain transactions. These blocks are chained together through "proof-of-work" mining, hence the term blockchain. This chaining of transactions in the correct timely order makes bitcoin unforgeable and immutable.

As soon as an actor in the Bitcoin network cheats, the network will detect and ban it temporarily. This means you don't need to trust anyone, there is no need for an intermediary like a bank or PayPal. This doesn't mean that there are no scammers out there or that you can stop verifying what is true or false, or stop learning about how to use Bitcoin. Knowledge is power.

Bitcoin's motto is "Don't trust, verify." This was a little bit confusing to me at the beginning. On the one hand, you learn that you don't have to trust an intermediary. Yet, on the other, you could verify your transactions. What it means is this: if you want to verify bitcoin transactions yourself, you can do so. In fact, if you have the technical knowledge to set up your own full node, you should verify.

This is revolutionary – as soon as you start to verify your own bitcoin transactions, you essentially become a bank. This is what banks do – they verify your transactions in their ledgers. However, you need to trust them to do a good job. That might be working very well in developed countries, but the banking experience is much worse for most parts of the world. Now imagine you do not have a reliable banking situation or an ID, but you do have a mobile phone and access to the internet. There is only one option for you to store and use money. It's either mobile money like M-Pesa or EcoCash in Africa or cryptocurrencies, where you do not need to identify yourself.

All people worldwide with an internet-enabled mobile phone have access to Bitcoin. The banks as we know them are not required for the use of Bitcoin. You don't have to ask anyone for permission to own or use Bitcoin. All you need to get started is a smartphone, an internet connection and a bitcoin wallet app.

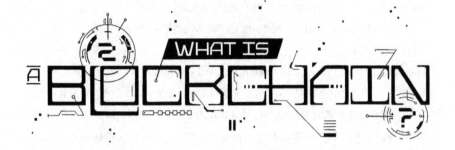

WHAT IS A BLOCKCHAIN?

The Bitcoin blockchain is a public, immutable database where all Bitcoin transactions are stored. Thus, "the blockchain" itself is not the revolutionary technological breakthrough as it is usually described in the media. As you learned in chapter I.4 "The History of Bitcoin", adding a blockchain was the element that finally solved the problem of double-spending and enabled the decentralized issuance of money on a secured decentralized network. Bitcoin has a lot of other preceding technology in it.

In fact, Satoshi Nakamoto never mentioned the word blockchain. Instead, Nakamoto used the term time chain, because the ledger's main use is to store all transactions in the correct chronological order.

Since the word blockchain has become the commonly used term, I will follow suit in using it here. Since it was created in 2009, the Bitcoin blockchain has never been hacked. Since 2009, every single transaction has been stored on the blockchain. Every transfer that has been made in Bitcoin since its inception is decentrally stored on an estimated 10,000 to 100,000 computers worldwide. These computers are run by individuals, universities, exchanges and so on. This decentralization makes it hard to attack Bitcoin because, if you attack

one computer and the blockchain, there are still thousands of identical databases acting as a consensus-based back-up. Attempting to introduce false transactions to the ledger will result in failure because the rest of the nodes around the world would fail to reach a consensus with the impostor node, rejecting its transaction record.

The data within the Bitcoin blockchain is transparent and public. If you make a transaction you can look it up in a Bitcoin explorer, which is like a search engine that trawls the database of transactions as opposed to web pages. You can see the value on a bitcoin address that is recorded on the blockchain. With your private keys – the blockchain equivalent of your password – you have access to your public address and can move the value on the blockchain to another address.

The Bitcoin blockchain belongs to no one, anyone can download it and store it on their own computer. With this "full node", you can also contribute to the strengthening of the Bitcoin network. Why? By verifying your own copy of the blockchain, you are not trusting anyone else to be honest with you. The more people who do this, the more distributed and robust the Bitcoin network becomes.

Open and Permissioned Blockchains

Please note the difference between Bitcoin, which is an open blockchain and, for instance, "Diem" (Facebook's money project token) or the Chinese government's E-Yuan CBDC, which are closed and centralized blockchains.

An open blockchain is accessible to all people, it is decentralized, transparent, uncensorable and neutral, making it the revolutionary money it is: a global, internet-native system that is open to everyone regardless of age, color, privilege, gender or nation. Bitcoin can even be used by machines. No one can keep you from sending it peer-to-peer around the world.

A permission-based, private blockchain, is closed, non-transparent, hierarchically organized and centrally stored. The company or government running the system can exclude and censor your transactions. They can close your account and keep you from spending your money. You're already familiar with this system because it's how the current traditional banking system works.

2.1 Bitcoin the Internet of Values

Bitcoin is more than a digital coin or internet-native money. It is a public internet infrastructure. It is an internet protocol through which values are exchanged between computers operated by humans, but also by autonomous machines themselves. For example, cars won't only drive autonomously in the future, but will also navigate to the charging station on their own for recharging. In this scenario, the payment is made automatically via bitcoin without anyone having to intervene manually.

A protocol governs the exchange of information or procedures. Language is a protocol. When I speak and take a short break, my counterpart knows that she can speak now. Every word in a conversation has a meaning, every expression changes the tone of a conversation. The human language protocol regulates the communication between two or more people. Computers also talk to each other. For example, their protocols are SMTP for email transmission, FTP for sending files, or HTTPS for visiting web pages. The respective protocol determines how data is exchanged with each other so that one computer can understand the other.

2.1.1 Internet Protocol Stack

The Bitcoin protocol can be compared to the structure of the internet protocol stack.

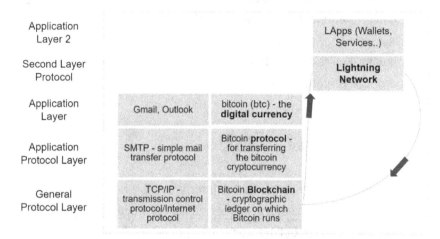

Bitcoin is a common good.

Source: Anita Posch inspired by Melanie Swan, https://www.slideshare.net/lablogga/bitcoin-and-blockchain-explained-cryptocitizen-smartnetwork-trust

The Bitcoin blockchain is a new internet protocol comparable to the TCP/IP protocol, which is the basis of the internet. On top of the Bitcoin blockchain, the Bitcoin protocol transfers bitcoin values similar to the SMTP protocol for sending emails. On top of that, there is bitcoin as an application comparable to email software such as Gmail or Outlook. This is called the base layer of Bitcoin.

2.1.2 The Lightning Network

On top of the base layer protocol, additional layers can be built, such as the Lightning Network, which has been operating since 2018. That is why it is called the second-layer or layer two protocol. The Lightning Network enables fast and small payments, which are necessary due to the restricted block size technically not possible on the Bitcoin base layer. It also brings more privacy while using bitcoin, since it operates through private payment channels between thousands of nodes. Lightning payments hop from one node to the other, making it impossible to know who the payment sender is. Applications like wallets, lending services and more are being built on top of the Lightning protocol, bringing Bitcoin's security properties with it.

2.2 How Are Bitcoin Created?

We were talking about protocols and mathematical rules that regulate how Bitcoin works. A set of rules define how bitcoin are created and circulated. These rules can only be changed through a majority consensus from all parties involved in the Bitcoin network. Individuals, institutions or governments cannot change the Bitcoin rules unilaterally.

In our current monetary system of fiat currencies, the creation of money is in the hands of central bankers. They are steering and controlling the output of banknotes and coins, as well as the amount of credit that commercial banks may lend out, determining the interest rate and thus influencing the value of each unit of money.

Bitcoin are created in a process called mining in a decentralized manner, out of the hands of people with agenda-driven political power. The term "mining" has been chosen because, similar to the extraction of gold, labor and energy input is required for the creation of bitcoin.

2.3 What Is Bitcoin Mining?

You don't need to understand how Bitcoin mining works to use Bitcoin, but if you are interested in the details, what miners do and how bitcoin comes into existence, read on.

2.3.1 Mining in Easy Words

Imagine you want to fill a museum with artwork made of jigsaw puzzles, where each puzzle will contribute to the visitor's experience. There are clear rules: only puzzles that are assembled correctly and have won a competition can be placed in the museum. You will select and give a reward to the child that finishes the most difficult puzzle first. You don't want the child to be able to cheat against others or know in advance which puzzle will win. Now you send 10,000 children all over the world the same jigsaw puzzle and they start putting it together piece by piece at the same time. The child who finishes putting together the pieces first wins the prize. They have proven that they put the work in and the completed puzzle is the proof.

The process of building the puzzle cannot be corrupted, wrong puzzle pieces cannot be inserted and the child who wins cannot be artificially selected. The fastest child wins the prize. These are the rules. You can only change the rules if the parents, the children, the puzzle designer and the museum − all participants in the puzzle's network − decide collectively to do so. Here, when we talk about the prize, we are metaphorically speaking about the creation of bitcoin.

That is more or less what proof-of-work is about. Thousands of computers worldwide solving mathematical riddles at the same time, showing that they put an amount of effort in and, at the same time, decentralizing the reward earnings so that no one can collude or predict which miner will be the next to add a block to the chain. The effort the miners put in to validate the transactions and form blocks not only proves their work but also secures the blockchain. You can not change the past – historical transactions – in the Bitcoin blockchain without spending a lot of money on infrastructure and electricity to re-write the blockchain. That is why attacks on the Bitcoin network are possible in theory but are very, very expensive in reality.

2.3.2 Mining in Detail

Imagine you're already using Bitcoin and have a Bitcoin wallet installed on your smartphone. You order a product on the internet, choosing bitcoin as payment. The site will show you its Bitcoin address and you will use your mobile wallet to send the required amount. Then the following happens:

Your wallet signs the transaction. It is then broadcast into the Bitcoin network and enters a pool of other unconfirmed transactions, which is called the Mempool. The payee receives your transaction and their full node validates the transaction. It still waits, however, for confirmation that the transaction has been successfully added to a block before determining finality. That is the moment when you see that your transaction has been sent in your wallet but is pending, meaning it's not yet finally settled on the blockchain. You have zero confirmations at this time.

At the same time, the miners receive your transaction in their node's Mempool as well. A Bitcoin miner is a specialized device called ASIC.

Its only task is to run the hashing algorithm and solve the mining puzzle as fast as possible. There are hundreds of thousands of them, decentralized around the world.

The miners also have the full node software running which validates your transaction, checking that all the protocol rules were followed and that you, as the payer, have enough bitcoin to pay for the transaction. If the answer to these checks is yes, they add the transaction to their block template. But first of all, when they generate a new block template, the miner inserts the so-called coinbase transaction that, if they win the mining race, will pay them 6.25 bitcoin as a reward. After constructing the coinbase transaction, the computers select transactions from the Mempool and add them into the previously generated block template.

At the same time, the hashing computers (ASICs) are beginning to solve the mathematical puzzle. They compete with all other mining computers worldwide. The hasher that solves the puzzle first broadcasts the block to its peer nodes, who verify it and relay it to their peers, and so on until every node on the network has verified and stored the block. After 99 more blocks are added to the blockchain, the winning miner is allowed to spend the previously created subsidy of 6.25 bitcoin.

The payee, in fact, their full node, receives the block and validates it again and then finally confirms your transaction. Your payment is now attached to the chain in a data block and is completed. You receive a confirmation in your Bitcoin wallet that the payment has reached the recipient. You see in your wallet that your transaction has 1 confirmation. About every 10 minutes a new block is created and added after the block containing your transaction. After six blocks the transaction is considered to be practically irreversible.

The time span that your transaction needs to be settled depends on the transaction fee you are selecting and paying. The higher the fee, the faster the miners will insert your transaction in a block, because they earn these fees in addition to the block reward of 6.25 bitcoin.

Why this mathematical puzzle? Proof-of-work is resource-intensive as computers require large amounts of power. This fact leads to criticism of Bitcoin in light of the climate changes that we humans have created in recent decades. Chapter 3.1.11 "Bitcoin's Ecological Footprint" deals with this question in more detail.

Why do we need to use so much electricity? The answer is security and decentralization. The need to put effort and energy into mining protects the data in the blockchain from manipulation and makes it immutable and uncensorable. No state nor organization can change the blockchain.

Since its creation in 2009, the Bitcoin blockchain has never been hacked. Around 18.74 million bitcoin have been created so far, currently worth over six hundred billion USD (June 2021). Whilst a successful hack of the Bitcoin network could result in the greatest value heist in human history, it would require at least 51% of Bitcoin mining power to be concentrated under one owner or conglomerate. This could allow a malicious party to generate new blocks faster than the other 49% of miners, meaning they could theoretically override the consensus. But such an attack cannot steal, redirect or spend bitcoin without signatures. The attackers could only try to double-spend their own bitcoin in the most recent blocks and cause denial-of-service disruptions on the creation of future blocks.

Additionally, if an attack on Bitcoin were ever to succeed, then the Bitcoin blockchain would split as it has done several times before.

Participants in the Bitcoin blockchain could opt to switch over to supporting the 'new' chain or continue to support the 'old' chain version. This split of versions due to inherent rules is known as a hard fork. The 2017 Bitcoin / Bitcoin Cash hard fork proved that this would not be detrimental to the legitimacy of the blockchain.

The second major function of mining is to ensure decentralization. On the one hand, to make money creation independent from central entities and human power-grabs such as central banks, and on the other hand, to ensure that no miner can gain advantage and manipulate the blockchain. The calculation task is difficult and at the same time, as with a raffle, it is a matter of luck which computer finds a valid solution first. As a result, it is not possible to predict who the winning computer will be, which makes it impossible to influence the blockchain. If you don't know who will be first, you can't manipulate it and earn the reward.

If you are thinking about starting to use bitcoin, rest assured that the blockchain is secured by mining and distributed identically on thousands of different computers. It is very, very secure. Your most important task is to self-custody your bitcoin and keep the private keys (your password) secure.

2.4 21 Million Bitcoin

Bitcoin are created, as described in the previous pages, when a mining computer solves a computational task and is the first to successfully attach the newly minted block to the chain.

Miners currently receive a premium of 6.25 bitcoin for this work. This reward is the incentive for miners to behave positively towards the Bitcoin network and not cheat to change transactions in their favor.

2.4.1 Halving

The Bitcoin rules stipulate that the reward for the miners will be halved every 210,000 blocks, roughly every four years. At the beginning this reward was 50 bitcoin. Since May 2020 it is 6.25 bitcoin. In 2024 this reward will be halved into 3.125 bitcoin per block. This event is commonly called the Halving.

Satoshi Nakamoto coded these halvings into the Bitcoin Core software. The output quantity decreases over time, resulting in a flattening supply curve.

`bitcoin/src/validation.cpp:1238`

```
1238   CAmount GetBlockSubsidy(int nHeight, const Consensus::Params& consensusParams)
1239   {
1240       int halvings = nHeight / consensusParams.nSubsidyHalvingInterval;
1241       // Force block reward to zero when right shift is undefined.
1242       if (halvings >= 64)
1243           return 0;
1244
1245       CAmount nSubsidy = 50 * COIN;
1246       // Subsidy is cut in half every 210,000 blocks which will occur approximately every 4 years.
1247       nSubsidy >>= halvings;
1248       return nSubsidy;
1249   }
```

The halving interval code in the Bitcoin Core software in C++

Andreas (BEWARE of giveaway scams!) ✔ @aanton... · May 4, 2020 ···
The C++ code (in Bitcoin Core client) that will make the "bitcoin halving" happen

Constant values:
nSubsidyHalvingInterval = 210,000
nHeight (at the time) = 630,000
COIN = 100,000,000 (satoshi)

Find it in github.com/bitcoin/bitcoin

Explanation by Andreas M. Antonopoulos

Source: Andreas M. Antonopoulos, https://twitter.com/aantonop/status/1257366095515848716?s=20

This algorithm tends to zero such that there will be a maximum of 21 million bitcoin. There are currently around 18.7 million in circulation. In 2140 all 21 million bitcoin will have been generated. Mining will continue and the miners will be rewarded solely with transaction fees. By that point, it is expected that Bitcoin as a network will have such high adoption that transaction fees alone will adequately facilitate fair reward for miners.

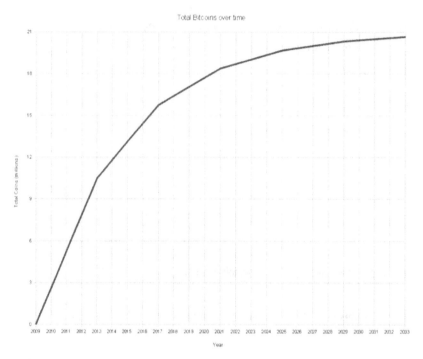

Total bitcoin supply over time

Source: Insti, https://commons.wikimedia.org/wiki/File:Total_bitcoins_over_time.png

2.4.2 Why 21 Million?

Why did Satoshi Nakamoto choose 21 million for the supply cap? There are many theories, but here is Satoshi's answer:

My choice for the number of coins and distribution schedule was an educated guess. It was a difficult choice, because once the network is going it's locked in and we're stuck with it. I wanted to pick something that would make prices similar to existing currencies, but without knowing the future, that's very hard. I ended up picking something in the middle. If Bitcoin remains a small niche, it'll be worth less per unit than existing currencies. If you imagine it being used for some fraction of world commerce, then there's only going to be 21 million coins for the whole world, so it would be worth much more per unit. Values are 64-bit integers with 8 decimal places, so 1 coin is represented internally as 100000000. There's plenty of granularity if typical prices become small. For example, if 0.001 is worth 1 Euro, then it might be easier to change where the decimal point is displayed, so if you had 1 Bitcoin it's now displayed as 1000, and 0.001 is displayed as 1.

Satoshi Nakamoto's explanation for the 21 million supply cap

Source: plan99.net, https://plan99.net/~mike/satoshi-emails/thread1.html

2.4.3 Bitcoin Units

The smallest denomination unit of a bitcoin is a satoshi. 1 bitcoin is comprised of 100,000,000 satoshis; 1 satoshi is one hundred millionth of 1 bitcoin (0.00000001).

You do not have to buy or sell 1 bitcoin at a time, you can start small and transact a minuscule fraction of it.

2.4.4 Bitcoin or bitcoin, but Never BitCoin

Bitcoin with a capital **B** is used when referring to the Bitcoin network, the blockchain, the community and the concept as a whole, whereas bitcoin with a lowercase b is used to reference the currency, the bitcoin token.

In fact, coin is the wrong term to describe the digital asset, it is a little bit misleading. In technical terms it is called UTXO – unspent transaction output. A UTXO defines the amount of value that is stored on the blockchain at a specific Bitcoin address. Therefore there are diverging opinions as to if there is a plural for bitcoin, the unit, because it's fluid and there are no set individual coins. But since Satoshi Nakamoto spoke of bitcoins, we as a community name it that way too. There is no plural for Bitcoin, as there is only one blockchain and network.

Scams like the BitClub network referred to it as BitCoin and this is often mistakenly used by Bitcoin beginners too.

2.5 Who Is Satoshi Nakamoto?

This puzzle may never be solved because there is no Satoshi Nakamoto. The name is a pseudonym. It could be an individual or a group of cryptographers, programmers and scientists. On August 18 2008, an unknown person registered the domain bitcoin.org. By registering the domain with the help of a company in Panama, the anonymity of the person is protected to this day.

On October 1 2008, Satoshi Nakamoto appeared on the "Cryptography Mailing List" and explained in a message that they had been working on an electronic cash system and posted the link to the Bitcoin white paper on https://bitcoin.org/bitcoin.pdf.

Hal Finney, an American cryptography and computer expert, had long been involved in the concept of digital money. However, none of the previous solutions were technically or conceptually mature enough to be used widely. The news from Satoshi Nakamoto sounded so interesting that Hal Finney started communicating with Nakamoto. On January 8, 2009, Nakamoto released the first version of the Bitcoin software. Five days earlier, on January 3, 2009, Nakamoto mined the first public bitcoin block, the so-called Genesis Block. Since then, on January 3, Bitcoin's birthday has been celebrated. Hal Finney was the first after Nakamoto to install the software on his computer and receive a transaction. Hal Finney sadly died of a nerve disease sometime later. Did he know who was hiding behind the pseudonym, Satoshi Nakamoto?

Until April 26 2011, Nakamoto participated in discussions about the Bitcoin network – they answered questions from other developers, explained new features of the software, and outlined some motives behind it. The last message (possibly) left by Satoshi Nakamoto was in March 2014 when a report about the alleged identification of the Bitcoin "inventor" went through the media. In San Francisco, Newsweek magazine tracked down Dorian Satoshi Nakamoto, an American of Japanese descent. It was claimed that he was the brains behind Bitcoin. With "I am not Dorian Nakamoto", the alleged Satoshi Nakamoto announced that Dorian was not "the" Satoshi Nakamoto.

If you have read this far, you have already invested time and energy in learning about Bitcoin. Why should or shouldn't you start to begin to use Bitcoin for yourself? Well, I advise you not to do so until you are sure that you want to try it. Only invest as much in Bitcoin as you understand and are comfortable to – only as much as you are willing to lose in a worst-case scenario.

The more you get to know and use Bitcoin, the more trust you will build. I researched the topic for three months before I installed my first bitcoin wallet and exchanged my first 75 euros for bitcoin. I want to help you to make up your own mind so will now discuss the most common arguments for and against Bitcoin.

3.1 Arguments Against Bitcoin

3.1.1 Volatility

Bitcoin is volatile, you cannot use it as a medium of exchange.

Yes, bitcoin price is volatile, it can lose or gain a lot of value in a single day. If you want to pay for something in bitcoin, you can still do so.

Just exchange the same amount you have spent from fiat back to bitcoin on the same day. No volatility, no loss or gain.

3.1.2 Price Development

Bitcoin is not a store of value due to its price changes.

View bitcoin as a long term investment, it has been the best performing store of value of all asset classes over the last decade.

@CharlieBilello	Asset Class Total Returns over Last 10 Years (as of 3/13/21)											Data Source: YCharts	
												2011-21	2011-21
ETF	Asset Class	2011	2012	2013	2014	2015	2016	2017	2018	2019	2020	2021 YTD	Cumulative	Annualized
N/A	Bitcoin (\$BTC)	1473%	186%	5507%	-58%	35%	125%	1331%	-73%	95%	301%	109%	20037142%	230.6%
QQQ	US Nasdaq 100	3.4%	18.1%	36.6%	19.2%	9.5%	7.1%	32.7%	-0.1%	39.0%	48.6%	0.5%	541.3%	20.0%
SPY	US Large Caps	1.9%	16.0%	32.2%	13.5%	1.2%	12.0%	21.7%	-4.5%	31.2%	18%	6.4%	282.4%	14.0%
IWM	US Small Caps	-4.4%	16.7%	38.7%	5.0%	-4.5%	21.6%	14.6%	-11.1%	25.4%	20.0%	19.1%	244.7%	12.9%
VNQ	US REITs	8.6%	17.6%	2.3%	30.4%	2.4%	8.6%	4.9%	-6.0%	28.9%	-4.7%	7.9%	147.7%	9.3%
TLT	Long Duration Treasuries	34.0%	2.6%	-13.4%	27.3%	-1.8%	1.2%	9.2%	-1.6%	14.1%	18.2%	-13.5%	88.7%	6.4%
PFF	Preferred Stocks	-2.0%	17.8%	-1.0%	14.1%	4.3%	1.3%	8.1%	-4.7%	15.9%	7.9%	-0.6%	76.3%	5.7%
EFA	EAFE Stocks	-12.2%	18.8%	21.4%	-5.2%	-1.0%	1.4%	25.1%	-13.8%	22.0%	7.6%	4.6%	76.3%	5.7%
HYG	High Yield Bonds	6.8%	11.7%	5.8%	1.9%	-5.0%	13.4%	6.1%	-2.0%	14.1%	4.5%	-0.2%	71.0%	6.4%
LQD	Investment Grade Bonds	9.7%	10.6%	-2.0%	8.2%	-1.3%	6.2%	7.1%	-3.8%	17.4%	11.0%	-6.4%	69.4%	5.3%
EMB	EM Bonds (USD)	7.7%	16.9%	-7.8%	6.1%	1.0%	9.3%	10.3%	-5.5%	15.5%	5.4%	-5.8%	62.4%	4.9%
TIP	TIPS	13.3%	6.4%	-8.5%	3.6%	-1.8%	4.7%	2.9%	-1.4%	8.3%	10.8%	-2.1%	40.3%	3.4%
EEM	EM Stocks	-18.8%	19.1%	-3.7%	-3.9%	-16.2%	10.9%	37.3%	-15.3%	18.2%	17.0%	4.5%	39.8%	3.3%
BND	US Total Bond Market	7.7%	3.9%	-2.1%	5.8%	0.6%	2.5%	3.6%	-0.1%	8.8%	7.7%	-3.7%	39.5%	3.3%
GLD	Gold	9.6%	6.6%	-28.3%	-2.2%	-10.7%	8.0%	12.8%	-1.9%	17.9%	24.8%	-9.5%	16.4%	1.5%
BIL	US Cash	0.0%	0.0%	-0.1%	-0.1%	-0.1%	0.1%	0.7%	1.7%	2.2%	0.4%	0.0%	4.8%	0.5%
DBC	Commodities	-2.6%	3.5%	-7.6%	-28.1%	-27.6%	18.6%	4.9%	-11.6%	11.8%	-7.8%	18.5%	-34.9%	-4.1%
	Highest Return	BTC	BTC	BTC	VNQ	BTC	BTC	BTC	BIL	BTC	BTC	BTC	BTC	BTC
	Lowest Return	EEM	BIL	GLD	BTC	DBC	BIL	BIL	BTC	BIL	DBC	TLT	DBC	DBC
	% of Asset Classes Positive	65%	94%	41%	65%	41%	100%	100%	6%	100%	88%	47%	94%	94%

Bitcoin the best asset over the 10 years prior 2021

Source: Charlie Bilello, https://twitter.com/charliebilello/status/1370722188739891202/photo/1

There is of course no guarantee that this performance will continue forever.

At the time of writing bitcoin was in a bull run, which started in the last quarter of 2020. This means that the price appreciated for a period of weeks and months with little setbacks in between. In May 2021 a significant drop occurred, which many interpreted as a healthy setback in an overheated market. The last bull run started in 2017 and ended at the beginning of 2018. Since then the price has moved relatively sideways – as it is called in traders terms – meaning that no particularly large movements in price have occurred, either up or down.

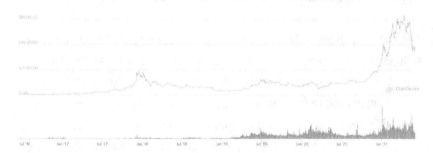

Bitcoin price development

Source: CoinGecko, https://www.coingecko.com/en/coins/bitcoin/usd, June 7, 2021

Bitcoin price development is following the halving cycles. Approximately every 4 years the amount of minted bitcoin is reduced by 50%. This means that the growth of available bitcoin on the market is shrinking. Even if the demand for bitcoin only remains at the same level, the price will increase.

3.1.3 Digital Scarcity

The total bitcoin supply is limited to 21 million, 18.7 million of which are already on the market. Every four years (exactly 210,000 blocks), the amount of bitcoin that is minted is reduced by half. Currently, the mining process generates 6.25 bitcoin every 10 minutes, which is 900 bitcoin per day and 328,500 per year. From 2024, there will only be 450 bitcoin minted per day, as only 3.125 bitcoin will be issued for each block generated. This means that the amount available every day decreases and supply becomes scarcer. If interest increases at the same time, the price rises exponentially.

As of May 2021, around 36 million USD (number of daily minted bitcoin * price) must flow into the Bitcoin market every day to keep the current price of 40,000 USD stable. Whenever the price drops, fewer bitcoin were exchanged than were available on that day and vice versa.

The dates of these halvings are annotated in the chart below. The price follows similar patterns before and after each halving. In this chart the top of bitcoin is predicted to be in September 2021, after which the price is expected to fall again as you can see on the "Low" marked grid lines. Of course, this is just a prediction based on a few historic events and numbers. We cannot take this as a given occurrence in the future.

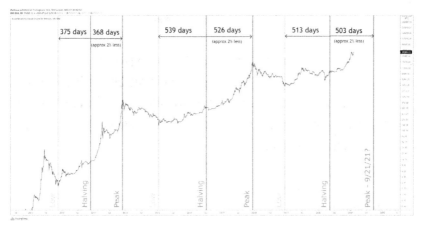

Halving price cycles

Source: Pladizow, https://twitter.com/Pladizow/status/1358545292782497792/photo/1

Since Bitcoin's launch in 2009, there have been several price crashes. Be prepared that this will happen again. The question is how low will it go because on a logarithmic scale you can see that, over time, bitcoin has only gained value in the long term.

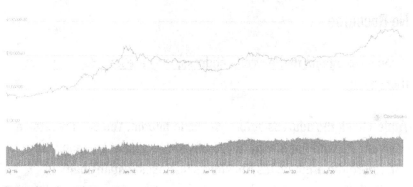

Bitcoin price logarithmic scale
Source: CoinGecko, https://www.coingecko.com/en/coins/bitcoin/usd, June 7, 2021

> Don't try to outsmart the market, don't trade. Just hold your bitcoin. At least for five years.

In the case of a bear market, when the price of bitcoin inevitably goes down, you will lose value in fiat money terms. However, your stack of bitcoin remains the same. If you hold 0.3 bitcoin in a bull market, you hold 0.3 bitcoin in a bear market too. Your losses are in your perception only, depending on what currency or asset you compare your bitcoin to on a given day. Be patient, wait, don't sell – history indicates that long-term holding is a sure way of protecting your value.

> Only put as much money into bitcoin as you are willing to lose. If you can't sleep in times of depreciation, then you might hold too much of a risky asset like bitcoin.

3.1.4 No Recourse

If you send bitcoin to the wrong address, they are lost. You can't get them back.

Triple-check the address before you send bitcoin. You can't reverse a payment. As with fiat money, if you buy something at an online store and return the product, it's the store's business responsibility to handle the bitcoin and send it back to you. However, a simple mistyping of an address should result in an error rather than lost funds, as addresses include integrity checks.

3.1.5 No Safety Net

In developed regions of the world, bank account deposits (in Europe up to 100,000 euro) are insured. This is not the case with bitcoin.

That's correct. If you self-custody your bitcoin, then you are solely responsible. There is no insurance. But be aware that, in case of a big financial crisis, these fiat insurances might not be able to pay you back anyhow. During the financial crisis in Cyprus in 2013, 47.5% of all bank deposits above 100,000 euro were seized. If you self-custody – nobody can seize your bitcoin.

If we open our eyes and think of the rest of the world, where 2 billion people are unbanked and 80% of the world's population live in authoritarian states, the case for an uncensorable money such as bitcoin, where you are in control and not a bank, makes logical sense again. In those countries, where people have no safety net at all, the Bitcoin network can give security.

3.1.6 I Can't Afford to Invest

I can't buy one bitcoin, it's too expensive.

That's ok, you don't have to. There is no minimum budget you need to use bitcoin. A bitcoin is divisible into extremely small units, much smaller than a cent. You can buy a fraction of a bitcoin and start to play around with 20 USD or less.

You can also earn bitcoin, but more about that in chapter 9 "Earn Bitcoin".

3.1.7 Bitcoin Will Fail Like the First Internet Companies

Bitcoin is a new technology. It is the first of its kind. When we compare this with the first computer companies in the 1980s or the internet platforms of the dot com boom, almost none survived. Bitcoin was the first blockchain on the market, it might go the same route.

Bitcoin has been the world's most widely used cryptocurrency since it originated in 2009. I agree, there are no assurances that it will continue that way. The market dominance of Bitcoin was over 80% until 2017. Meaning that, of all the thousands of cryptocurrencies on the market, over 80% of all investments were held in Bitcoin. This changed in 2017-18 when there was a "war" between different ideas around how Bitcoin as a technology should go forward. The block-size debate ended with a hard-fork, where the Bitcoin blockchain split into two forks: Bitcoin (BTC) and Bitcoin Cash (BCH). At that time, other crypto projects like Ethereum gained importance. Four years later, BCH has steadily declined into insignificance compared to BTC. Bitcoin held its dominance with over 60% until the current bull run, where it dropped

to 40% by the time of writing. A bull run results in more mainstream attention, which leads to many uninformed media articles and when certain billionaires add rumors and speculation to the mix, Altcoins are lifted into focus.

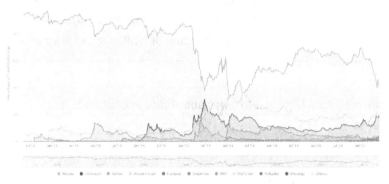

Percentage of total market capitalization

Source: CoinMarketCap, https://coinmarketcap.com/charts/, June 7, 2021

The resurgence of Bitcoin's dominance after the critical time of the hard-fork in 2017 was a sign of strength for many experts like macro-economist Lyn Alden and US investor Michael Saylor, which led them to believe in the future potential of Bitcoin as the winner-takes-all cryptocurrency. And even if there were technological innovations in Altcoins that would propel them in front of Bitcoin, there is no doubt that the Bitcoin developers would implement them too.

3.1.8 Bitcoin Has Failed

There are only a few Bitcoin users. After 12 years of existence, many more people should use Bitcoin. Bitcoin has failed.

Since the use of Bitcoin is, in principle, not tied to identities, it is not statistically possible to know how many people really use Bitcoin. Also, the number of Bitcoin addresses gives us no idea how many people use it. One person can have millions of addresses, or in the case of bitcoin on centralized exchanges, thousands of people can be managed by one large custodial address only.

Those centralized exchanges have to verify your identity before you are allowed to change fiat into bitcoin. The following statistic shows that over 101 million people around the world have an account at such an exchange. The people who managed to get some bitcoin in the early days, or operate outside the bounds of centralized exchanges go unaccounted for.

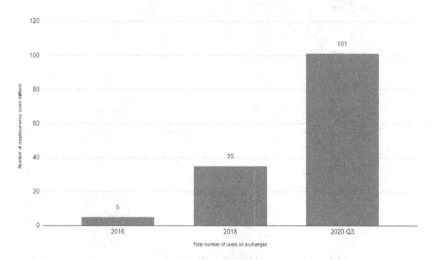

Number of identity-verified crypto asset users in millions

Source: Anita Posch, Source Cambridge Center for Alternative Finance, 3rd Global Cryptoasset Benchmarking Study, Fig. 34, https://www.jbs.cam.ac.uk/faculty-research/centres/alternative-finance/publications/3rd-global-cryptoasset-benchmarking-study

Around 1.3% of the world's population had an account at a cryptocurrency exchange at the end of 2020, a growth of nearly 190% between 2018 and 2020. Still, one could argue that this is not much. However, for a completely new asset class and money that originated as a grassroots movement without a company or marketing behind it,

Bitcoin has developed itself to the point where it is widely known, discussed and used by over at least 100 million people worldwide.

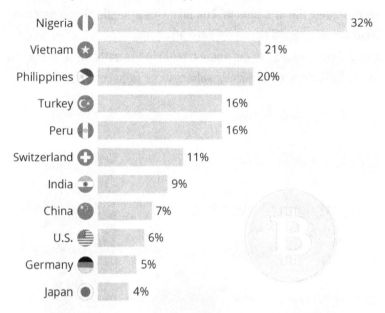

How Common Is Crypto?

Share of respondents in selected countries who said that they used or owned crypto currencies (2020)

Country	Percentage
Nigeria	32%
Vietnam	21%
Philippines	20%
Turkey	16%
Peru	16%
Switzerland	11%
India	9%
China	7%
U.S.	6%
Germany	5%
Japan	4%

1,000-4,000 respondents per country. Representative of online population.
Source: Statista Global Consumer Survey

Respondents who said they used or owned cryptocurrencies 2020

Source: Statista, https://www.statista.com/chart/18345/crypto-currency-adoption/

This is the result of a survey in selected countries showing that 32% of the Nigerian population has used or owns cryptocurrency. Keep in mind, the Nigerian population is on average 19 years old, compared to the US figure of 38 and Germany's median age of 44 years. They are young, want to work, are tech-savvy and value cryptocurrencies, despite their volatility, because their own national currency Naira is losing 25% of its value per year.

Want to know more about Bitcoin in Nigeria? Open your browser and go to: https://anita.link/88, https://anita.link/66 and https://anita.link/63

3.1.9 Bitcoin's Transaction Limit

The Bitcoin network is only capable of processing seven transactions per second. That is not enough to maintain a global payment network. If all people were using Bitcoin, the network would be overburdened.

The Lightning Network has been in development since the beginning of 2018. This is a protocol that is located one level above the Bitcoin blockchain. The Lightning Network is expected to handle thousands of micro-payments per second in a few years and has already shown a good degree of success for instant cross-continent payments. The Bitcoin blockchain will be used as the base settlement layer for large transactions, while small payments for a coffee, for instance, will take place on the Lightning Network. As the user, you do not need to know how this works. Most of us do not know how Netflix or sending an email works and yet we do it every day.

3.1.10 Mining Pool Concentration

A mining pool is a structure that "pools" together computational resources provided by connected hashers (pool contributors) to increase the likelihood of finding a new block, which results in more bitcoin reward pay-outs.

While it is true that mining pools can become concentrated in specific areas or jurisdictions, like in China before their authoritarian government outlawed Bitcoin mining in June 2021, they still have less influence than you may first think. Firstly, mining pools consist of thousands of individual miners. Just because a mining pool is located in China does not mean that the individual miner has to be located in China. Hashers want to ensure that the pool they contribute to is engaging in behavior that is aligned to the Bitcoin philosophy. In an event of disagreement, miners are free to switch pools. In 2013, the Bitcoin mining pool GHash.io reached more than 50% of the total Bitcoin hashrate for a short period, which prompted hashers to proactively point their hashpower to other pools in order to avoid potentially harmful concentration. The low cost of switching pools acts as a system of checks and balances on the self-regulating behavior of miners.[2]

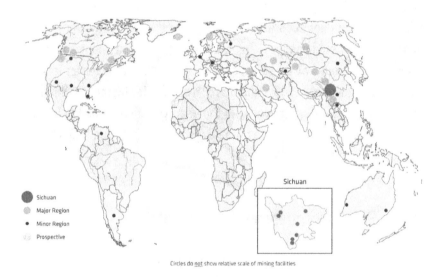

Circles do not show relative scale of mining facilities

Global Overview of Bitcoin Mining Regions. Regions With Large Relevant Regions Shown in Teal, Sichuan in Blue and Remaining Minor Regions in Black

Source: CoinShares, Bitcoin Mining, Dec. 2019, https://coinshares.com/de/research/bitcoin-mining-network-december-2019

2 2nd global cryptoasset benchmarking study, https://www.jbs.cam.ac.uk/faculty-research/centres/alternative-finance/publications/2nd-global-cryptoasset-benchmark-study/

The 2017 hard-fork split between Bitcoin and Bitcoin Cash is a second example of how Bitcoin is self-regulating. Miners and big exchanges wanted to increase the block size of each Bitcoin block to achieve a higher transaction output per block. The community of node operators and Bitcoin users did not want to change the block size because people with lower bandwidth would have been disadvantaged. Instead, they opted for 2nd layer solutions like the Lightning Network to address this problem. This resulted in the "Blocksize war", where miners and big companies tried to force the changes upon the network. This resulted in a hard-fork: Bitcoin split into Bitcoin and Bitcoin Cash. Four years later, Bitcoin Cash is almost forgotten, while Bitcoin is the largest cryptocurrency. It shows that miners do not have more power than other users.

3.1.11 Bitcoin's Ecological Footprint

<u>Bitcoin consumes a lot of electricity, which will increase our climate crisis and is irresponsible.</u>

TECH & SCIENCE

Bitcoin Mining on Track to Consume All of the World's Energy by 2020

BY **ANTHONY CUTHBERTSON** ON 12/11/17 AT 10:07 AM EST

Newsweek article from 2017

Source: Newsweek, 12/11/2017, https://www.newsweek.com/bitcoin-mining-track-consume-worlds-energy-2020-744036

The above screenshot is an article from Newsweek right in the middle of the 2017-2018 bull run. It is based on the work of Alex de Vries (Digiconomist), a former data analyst for the Dutch Central Bank. Many research papers and mainstream media articles are based on his false assumptions, like comparing Bitcoin transactions' energy consumption to VISA payments and calculating a carbon footprint from this. I argue that a lot of this work is done to spread false claims in order to demonize Bitcoin.

> "Every time we have a rally in Bitcoin we see all of this negative attention to the environmental impact of Bitcoin. Apparently it only matters when the price is high." – ANDREAS M. ANTONOPOULOS

Let's dive into this. Bitcoin critics often mention that Bitcoin's energy consumption outweighs the benefits it creates. It's undeniable that Bitcoin mining requires lots of electricity. It is estimated that between 80 and 118 TWh per year are used globally for mining which is equivalent to the entire power consumption of countries like the Netherlands.

Country ranking, March 2021
Source: Cambridge Center for Alternative Finance, March 2021, https://cbeci.org/cbeci/comparisons/

The world wastes a lot of electricity. The amount of electricity consumed every year by always-on but inactive home devices in the USA alone could power the Bitcoin network for 1.9 years. This means that the amount of energy wasted in the USA could almost power the Bitcoin network twice over, year-on-year.[3]

At the same time, two-thirds of all energy produced in the USA is lost. It's reasonable to assume that this is happening in all other parts of the world too.

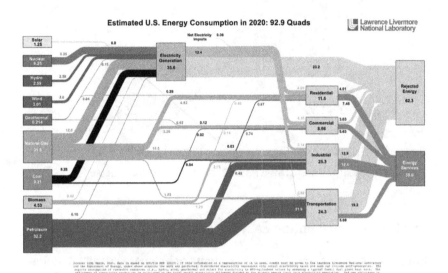

Estimated US Energy Consumption in 2017 – Rejected Energy

Source: Energy Flow Chart, Lawrence Livermore National Laboratory, https://flowcharts.llnl.gov/

Notice that rejected energy accounts for around 62% of all electricity generation. Rejected energy is energy that is produced but ultimately does not go towards useful work. To make matters worse, over time, this number has been increasing on a relative basis. In 1970 Lawrence Livermore National Laboratory found our proportion of rejected energy was around 48%.[4]

To put it another way, Bitcoin accounts for 0.54% of all electricity used globally.

---

3 Source Cambridge Center for Alternative Finance, March 2021, https://cbeci.org/cbeci/comparisons/

4 Conner Brown, Bitcoin: a bold american future, https://journal.bitcoinreserve.com/bitcoin-a-bold-american-future/

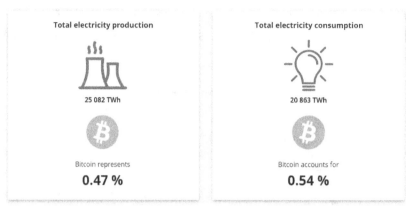

The world's total electricity production, consumption and Bitcoin's share, March 2021[5]

Source: Cambridge Center for Alternative Finance, March 2021, https://cbeci.org/cbeci/comparisons/

Electricity Consumption Easy to Quantify

Bitcoin's transparency allows estimations of its energy demand, quite in contrast to many other industries where these data points are more obscure. Measured by electricity costs alone, we can assume that, on a global scale, Bitcoin is much more efficient (https://medium.com/@danhedl/pow-is-efficient-aa3d442754d3) than traditional banking and gold mining.

Bitcoin mining's estimated dollar cost per Gigajoule expended is 40 times more efficient than that of traditional banking and 10 times more efficient than that of gold mining.

---

5 Cambridge Center for Alternative Finance

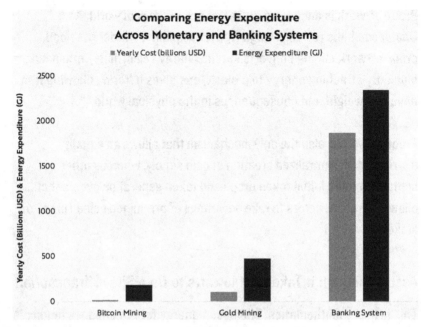

Comparing energy expenditure across monetary and banking systems

Source: ARK Invest, Bitcoin myths, https://ark-invest.com/articles/analyst-research/bitcoin-myths/

Why Does Bitcoin Need This Amount of Electricity?

The proof-of-work mining mechanism is a fundamental feature that secures the independence, neutrality and automated integrity of the network. It is the most secure way to prevent attacks on the assets worth over 600 billion USD that are locked in the network. (BTC market cap, June 2021)

Bitcoin can settle transactions without intermediaries because specialized, dedicated hardware proves transparently that the computer has executed a costly computation.

Proof-of-work is anchoring digital money in the real world. As Chaincode Labs resident Hugo Nguyen explains, "Under the hood, proof-of-work mining converts kinetic energy (electricity) into a ledger block. By attaching energy to a block, one gives it 'form', allowing it to have real weight and consequences in the physical world."[6]

Proof-of-work is also the only mechanism that allows an equally distributed, decentralized creation of coin supply, whereas other methods require initial token drops and token generation events that allow centralized actors to take advantage of pre-mined coins (proof-of-stake).

Assumption #1: It Takes X Kilowatts to Do a Single Transaction

This is faulty mathematics. The use of energy for bitcoin does not scale to the number of transactions. The number of transactions that happen on-chain and the number of transactions that happen off-chain – for instance, on second-layer technologies like the Lightning Network or through custodial exchanges, that batch transactions – are not correlated at all to the cost of mining. 80-90% of mining is driven by bitcoin's price, with the other 10-20% being driven by fees. The higher the possible profit for miners, the more chance that miners will set up new mining facilities and when the price crashes, some will have to stop their machines. In the long term, when all 21 million bitcoin have been mined, the transaction fees alone will drive mining. At that point, transaction intensity will be more correlated to energy usage. But not today. The last bitcoin will be mined in 2140. Mining is driven by competition in a free market where mining difficulty adjusts dynamically. It has nothing to do with how many transactions are being processed. Mining is a mechanism for security. It relates to how much

---

6 ARK Invest Bitcoin myths, https://ark-invest.com/articles/analyst-research/bitcoin-myths/

security the market allocates to the system, so more energy equals more security and when the price of bitcoin goes up the amount of money allocated to protect it also increases naturally. Therefore, usage and higher adoption drive additional financial motivation for miners to produce more security by consuming more energy.

Assumption 2: Linear Extrapolation

The second wrong assumption is to extrapolate linearly and say that, if it takes X kilowatts of energy to make one transaction today and we have seven and a half billion people on the planet who will want to make one transaction per day each, then bitcoin's energy consumption in the future will be Y. This is false. Bitcoin can't scale linearly in terms of transactions because of block size constraints on the base layer. To mitigate that, second-layer protocols like the Lightning Network or sidechains like Liquid are developed, which allow thousands of payments without the need for extra energy. The efficiency of mining equipment is rising. Miners need less power for the same amount of computing performance over time. Additionally, Bitcoin developers are improving the code, minimizing the data size of transactions so that more transactions can be mined in one block.

Assumption 3: Comparing VISA to Bitcoin

A Bitcoin on-chain transaction cannot be compared with a VISA payment. It is not the same. In traditional banking there are various layers of settlement, meaning they differ in their level of security and finalization. Let's take the example of the US system, which is comparable globally. The base layer is Fedwire, CHIPS and SWIFT networks, while debit card and credit card payments operate one or two levels above with many intermediaries. The base layer of Bitcoin has to be compared with Fedwire, CHIPS and SWIFT. Only second-layer

solutions like fast, micropayments on the Lightning Network can be compared with VISA.

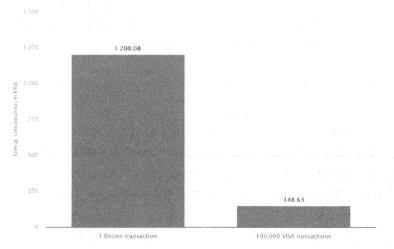

False comparison between a bitcoin transaction and VISA

Source: Statista, https://www.statista.com/statistics/881541/bitcoin-energy-consumption-transaction-comparison-visa/

Let's take a look at the average transaction volume of VISA and Bitcoin.

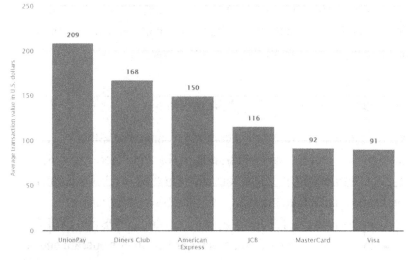

Average value of a single credit card transaction worldwide in 2012, USD

Source: Statista, https://www.statista.com/statistics/279308/average-credit-card-transaction-value-worldwide/

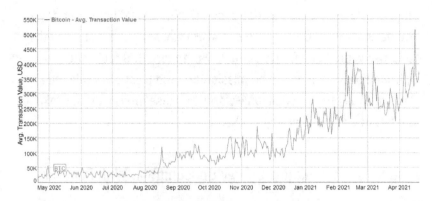

Average value of a single Bitcoin transaction

Source: BitInfoCharts, https://bitinfocharts.com/comparison/bitcoin-transactionvalue.html#1y

The average bitcoin transaction value was 258,766 USD on April 21st, 2021, while the average VISA transaction was 91 USD in 2012. Bitcoin transactions transport magnitudes more value in comparison to credit card payments. Assuming Bitcoin gains mass adoption then it might one day settle millions of dollars worth like the Fedwire system at very low fees compared to the banking system.

The average transaction value per Fedwire transfer was 4.5 million USD in February 2021.

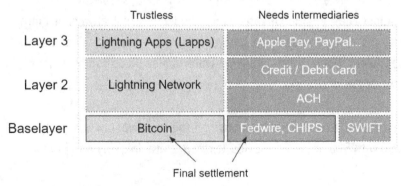

Settlement of banking versus Bitcoin

Source: Anita Posch

Bitcoin transactions are settled every 10 minutes, 24 hours per day, 365 days per year. Compare this to ACH transactions which can take up to two years to be finally settled.[7] Not to forget: Bitcoin and Lightning transactions are permissionless and trustless while the traditional payment system only works because intermediaries take custody of fraud and chargebacks.

Assumption 4: Equating Energy Consumption With Pollution

People say, for example, that "every transaction pollutes" or "bitcoin's pollution is increasing" or "bitcoin produces pollution as a result of its energy consumption" – that's simply not true. There is no direct correlation between energy usage and pollution because it depends entirely on what type of energy is being used. If you're producing energy with coal, that causes pollution and environmental impact. If you're producing energy with hydroelectric dams or wind or solar for example, then you're not actually polluting. In fact, you're subsidizing those energy mechanisms and incentivizing the creation of more solar, wind, geothermal, off-gassing and other forms of energy through the application of bitcoin as an economic factor in the production of that energy.

Bitcoin miners are profit-driven, so they will always look for the cheapest energy, which is renewable. Coal and oil will always be more expensive than hydroelectric, geothermal, stranded gas, wind and solar power. Not to forget nuclear, which is also an option that many count as green energy.

Indisputably, Bitcoin miners are using otherwise wasted energy. I spoke with Sébastien Gouspillou (https://anita.link/101) and Philippe

---

7 Caitlin Long, https://twitter.com/CaitlinLong_/status/1384925713648734212?s=20

Bekhazi (https://anita.link/I03), two miners using hydropower, who confirmed the above statements.

Energy Mix of Electricity Production

Bitcoin miners are fairly well distributed across the globe. While it is easy to quantify the electricity demand, it is more difficult to quantify the electricity sources, since the Bitcoin mining industry remains a highly private and pseudonymous industry. Therefore, research on the electricity used in mining estimates renewable energy usage varies from 39% (Cambridge Center, CBECI.org) to 73% in the CoinShares Mining Whitepaper, which concludes:

"Using a combination of estimates of global mining locations and regional renewables penetrations we again calculate the Bitcoin mining industry to be heavily renewables-driven. Our current approximate percentage of renewable power generation in the Bitcoin mining energy mix stands at 73%, around four times the global average. Overall, our findings reaffirm our view that Bitcoin mining is acting as a global electricity buyer of last resort and therefore tends to cluster around comparatively under-utilised renewables infrastructure. This could help turn loss making renewables projects profitable and in time – as the industry matures and settles as permanent in the public eye – could act as a driver of new renewables developments in locations that were previously uneconomical."[8]

The question is not how much energy is required, but how is electricity produced? How much CO_2 is emitted? If we decide as a society that we

---

8 CoinShares, Bitcoin Mining Whitepaper 2019, https://coinshares.com/research/bitcoin-mining-network-december-2019

don't want polluting energy, then we should regulate the production of energy and not allow the use of polluting systems. This is about regulating energy production and not about regulating the consumption of energy in one particular sector of the economy which happens to be Bitcoin.

Bitcoin uses a higher amount of electricity from renewables than the grid in China, the USA and the wider world.

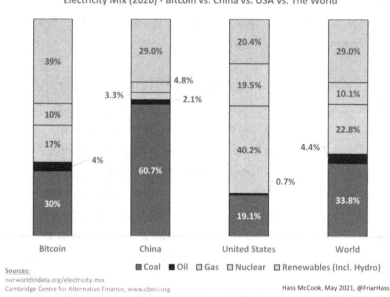

Electricity Mix, Bitcoin vs. China vs. USA vs. The World, 2020
Source: Hass McCook, https://bitcoinmagazine.com/business/what-elon-musk-gets-wrong-about-bitcoin

Carbon Emissions

Some research has tried to assess the carbon emission flows and sustainability of Bitcoin through estimating future demand, based on false assumptions. One paper for instance is claiming that: "the annual energy consumption of the Bitcoin blockchain in China is expected to peak in 2024 at 296.59 Twh and generate 130.50 million metric tons of carbon emission correspondingly."[9]

> "It's an immediate red flag that the authors confidently declare Bitcoin's future carbon outlay to two decimal places, when realistically the number can only be estimated to within an order of magnitude.", states Nic Carter.[10]

Based on the work of Hass McCook (https://bitcoinmagazine.com/business/bitcoin-vs-financial-sector-energy-use) Bitcoin emits less than 2% of the world's military-industrial complex and less than 5% of the legacy financial sector's carbon emissions. The annual global greenhouse gas emissions are approx. 50,000 million ton carbon dioxide equivalent. Bitcoin emits only 0.11% of those.

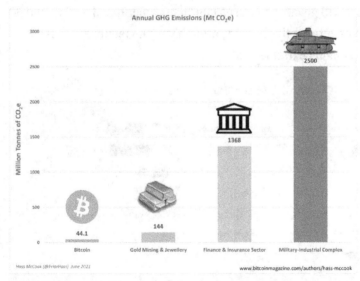

Annual Greenhouse Gas Emissions, Hass Mc Cook, June 2021

Source: Annual Greenhouse Gas Emissions, Hass McCook, June 2021, https://bitcoinmagazine.com/culture/bitcoin-vs-world-military-emissions

9   Nature communications, https://www.nature.com/articles/s41467-021-22256-3

10 Nic Carter, On Bitcoin, the Gray Lady Embraces Climate Lysenkoism, https://medium.com/@nic__carter/on-bitcoin-the-gray-lady-embraces-climate-lysenkoism-a2d31e465ec0

Final Assumption: Bitcoin Isn't Useful, Therefore Any Use of Energy for a Bitcoin is Wasteful

If you decide Bitcoin isn't useful, then this is a very subjective opinion. Bitcoin might not make sense to you, but it might make sense for many other people. If you are making this argument, you must agree that there are many other forms of energy use that are prima facie useless or even damaging in their use, and they don't receive the same amount of scrutiny.

We can light up billions of Christmas lights every year for a display of Christmas spirit, which might be completely pointless for billions of people of other beliefs. The number one use of energy in the United States, for example, outside of civilian markets is the Department of Defense. The US government uses enormous amounts of energy and is the largest polluter in the country, arguably for no legitimate reason other than seeking extreme control.

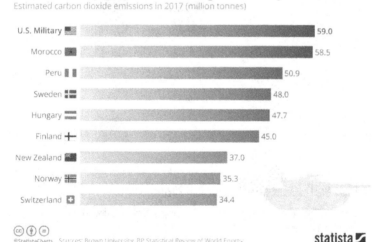

US military emits more CO2 than many nations

Source: Statista, https://www.statista.com/chart/18359/estimated-military-carbon-dioxide-emissions/

This leads back to the chapter about the Petrodollar, the linkage between the US dollar and the OPEC, which makes the USA the globally dominant powerhouse and is secured by the US military and wars in the Gulf region.

Is the war machine a useful thing to have in our society? Before you scream "Whataboutism!", say that it's comparing two different things and demand we should reduce the use of the war machine as well as the use of bitcoin, do not forget there's a very important link that is missing. The war machine all around the world is funded directly by fiat debt that is produced and paid off through inflation that is enabled through the uncontrolled central bank printing money, which in the end you, the taxpayer, are fronting the bill for. Bitcoin isn't just a solution for an open economy, it's a solution that constrains governments from producing currency at unreasonable rates and using inflation as a hidden form of taxation to fund the war machine, which ultimately pollutes and damages more than anything else in existence. Bitcoin isn't simply a substitute for general economic activity, it's also a direct control on the war machine that pollutes and uses far more energy simply to kill people. So, in my opinion, those two things are very closely tied. But that's just Andreas M. Antonopoulos' and my own opinion.

Conclusion: The Benefits of Bitcoin

Bitcoin is uncensorable, incorruptible, and allows billions of people open access to a global money system, regardless of color, gender, wealth, and status. Furthermore, it is our only chance to secure financial privacy, or at least pseudonymity, in a world of digital surveillance.

The Bitcoin network secures assets for about 100 million users globally, worth over 600 billion USD (June 2021) without any upper limit and does not rely on military power or currency wars.

Here is a conclusion, as put by ARK Invest: "Contrary to consensus thinking, we believe the environmental impact of bitcoin mining is de minimis. Renewables, particularly hydroelectric power, accounts for a large percentage of bitcoin's energy mix. As Castle Island Ventures partner, Nic Carter, has noted, in their search for the cheapest form of electricity, miners will continue to flock to regions offering a glut of renewable electricity, unlocking stranded energy assets as 'electricity buyer's of last resort, creating a highly mobile base-demand for any electricity sources able to produce at prices below current producers, regardless of location.' As a result, from a climate perspective, bitcoin mining could be a net positive."[II]

3.2 Arguments for Bitcoin

> "Bitcoin is an opt-in system. You choose to use it. You choose what apps you're going to run. You choose who you're going to interact with. You choose the rules of the game by which you're going to interact. That's why bitcoin is going to win. It delivers innovation that consumers want and need." – ANDREAS M. ANTONOPOULOS

3.2.1 A Paradigm Shift

I'm a digital native individual in a Gen X body. I can remember life without the internet, even without a VCR. We had one TV station in Austria, that was it. My parents got our first landline phone when I was 12. At 14 I used my first computer, in 1997 I installed my first internet connection and email at home. That same year there were only 1 million websites globally and Google and Amazon did not exist internationally.

II ARK Invest Bitcoin myths, https://ark-invest.com/articles/analyst-research/bitcoin-myths/

A lot of people dismissed the internet as a trend that would go away. In 1995, US astronomer and author Clifford Stoll wrote an article for Newsweek titled "The Internet? Bah!"

> "Then there's cyberbusiness. We're promised instant catalog shopping – just point and click for great deals. We'll order airline tickets over the network, make restaurant reservations and negotiate sales contracts. Stores will become obsolete. So how come my local mall does more business in an afternoon than the entire Internet handles in a month? Even if there were a trustworthy way to send money over the Internet – which there isn't – the network is missing a most essential ingredient of capitalism: salespeople." – CLIFFORD STOLL[12]

Fast forward to 2019 and Amazon is in the top ten biggest companies in the world, Google and YouTube are the biggest search engines and there are 1.8 billion active websites. My first contact with Bitcoin and blockchains was in April 2017 when I heard a talk by Shermin Voshmgir. It clicked immediately. 20 years after I changed my career from being an urban planner to becoming an internet entrepreneur, I understood that Bitcoin is as massive as the dawn of the internet in 1997.

The discovery of Bitcoin was the advent of a new technology on top of the internet that we use for media and communication. The internet of money, which allows us to exchange value globally without boundaries. Communication over the internet has changed the world massively in the last few decades. What do you think the impact of the free movement of value will have? Bitcoin and other open, public digital assets will shift the power dynamics between nations since it is suddenly possible to move huge amounts of money at speed, without friction or touching the current financial system.

---

12 Clifford Stoll, https://www.newsweek.com/clifford-stoll-why-web-wont-be-nirvana-185306

Bitcoin is a new technology. If we compare its development to the internet, we are pretty much where the internet was in 1997.

3.2.2 Enabling Social Change

People in developed nations with functioning democratic systems often dismiss Bitcoin as a tool for speculation and a danger for nation-states. Therefore, some think its electricity consumption is environmentally irresponsible. Some even advocate for a ban. Expect this kind of criticism to increase in the coming years.

The world's population is 7.8 billion people. Only 8.4% of those live in full democracies, 41% in flawed democracies, 15% in hybrid regimes and 35.6% in authoritarian regimes.

Over 50% of the world's population are living in nations far from free and fair democracies! 1.7 billion people do not have a bank account and never will. Bitcoin is for them.[13]

It's people in regions like Africa and South America who will drive Bitcoin adoption forward. The main use-cases there are:

Hedge Against Inflation

This table by the International Monetary Fund shows the annual change of consumer prices in percent.

---

13 Wikipedia, Democracy Index, https://en.wikipedia.org/wiki/Democracy_Index

Venezuela	5.5 thousand
Sudan	197.1
Zimbabwe	99.3
Suriname	52.1
South Sudan, Republic of	40
Iran	39
Yemen	30.6
Angola	22.3
Haiti	20.5
Libya	18.2
Zambia	17.8
Nigeria	16
Sierra Leone	15.5
Turkey	13.6

Inflation rate, average consumer prices, annual change in %[14]

Source: International Monetary Fund, Inflation rate, https://www.imf.org/external/datamapper/PCPIPCH@WEO/OEMDC/ADVEC/WEOWORLD, requested on April 26th, 2021

- **Venezuela saw prices increases by 5,500%. The suffering of the people is simply incomprehensible.**
- **In Sudan the prices increased 200% in 2021 alone.**
- **Zimbabweans faced a doubling of prices at 100% inflation from 2020 to 2021.**
- **The IMF did not have data for Argentina, but I was informed by my Argentinian interview partner, Franco Amati, the annual inflation rate was 50%.**

---

14 International Monetary Fund

- Nigeria saw an inflation rate of 16% in 2020.
- Turkey's inflation rate in 2020 was 13.6 %.

From May 2020 to April 2021 the bitcoin trading volume in Nigeria increased by 40% from $287 million to $399 million. A 2020 survey shows that 32% of Nigerians who were interviewed had used or owned cryptocurrencies. Meanwhile, in developed democratic countries like Germany and the USA, only 5-6% have used or owned cryptocurrencies.

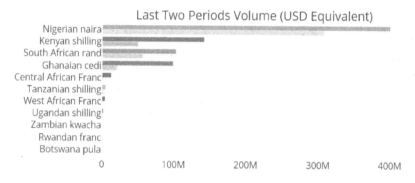

Trading volume on P2P Bitcoin exchanges in Sub-Saharan countries from May 2020 to April 2021[15]
Source: https://www.usefultulips.org/combined_Sub%20Saharan%20Africa_Page.html, requested on April 26th, 2021

Given these annual inflation rates, people know that they need to store their wealth in harder money like USD, and better still, Bitcoin. If you explain the differences of Bitcoin to local currencies in these countries, everybody understands immediately how and why Bitcoin can support them.

---

15 Trading volume on P2P Bitcoin exchanges in Sub-Saharan countries from May 2020 to April 2021

Foreign Exchange Controls

Countries with weak economies and flawed democracies use foreign exchange controls to limit – what they call – speculation against their weak currencies. Since authoritarian leaders want to limit and control people's possibilities to circumvent their oppressive systems, they apply regulations such as the following:

- Argentina's capital controls only allow people to exchange a maximum amount of $200 per month from Argentine Pesos to USD.
- Quite the same harsh regulations apply in Zimbabwe. If you run a business and need to import goods you must ask the Reserve Bank for permission to send USD abroad. "Suppose I'm in solar power and I want to buy 20 panels so that I can sell them. I only have 30 days to spend down on the money that I already had. The Reserve Bank can take as long as it wants to give me permission to even go and resupply. That's another reason why the US actual physical dollars, the physical cash has so much more value in Zimbabwe", a Zimbabwean interview partner told me in March 2020.

Banking System Is Not Available or Broken

- Local businesses in Zimbabwe are allowed to use USD to bill a local supplier. That supplier has to liquidate those US dollars within 30 days, or the money gets converted into their RTGS account at the bank rate. RTGS is the name for the Zimbabwean dollar, which shows these high inflation rates.
- If you buy foreign currency at an Argentinian bank the official bank exchange rate is used (which is favorable for the bank, but not the customer) and on top of that a 65% tax is deducted.

- Using the banking system can be full of red tape in Western countries too, but it's much worse in those countries.

Remittances

- If you receive money from abroad through the traditional banking system it will be converted to Argentine pesos at the official bank rate. This basically represents a confiscation of 30% of the value.
- In 2020 as much as I billion USD have been sent as remittances to Zimbabwe. Over one-third of the population relies on remittances from relatives abroad. A lot of Zimbabweans live in South Africa and of the money they send, up to 20-30% are lost through banking fees and official exchange rates.[16]

Barriers for Women

Using a basic bank account is beyond the reach of almost one billion women worldwide. Varying degrees of gender inequality permitted or mandated by law deny women full financial participation in many countries around the world. Depending on the country, women are discriminated against in inheritance laws and are required to obtain their husband's permission to legally work, get a bank account, register a business or sign a contract; many women are banned from entering certain professions. Women may also find it more difficult to access legal ID cards due to existing laws or restrictive registration requirements, and such identification is commonly required to use financial products and services.

---

16 World Bank, Sending money from South Africa to Zimbabwe, https://remittanceprices.worldbank.org/en/corridor/ South-Africa/Zimbabwe, requested on April 26th, 2021

Other hurdles that prevent women from accessing financial services are the need to travel long distances, the risk of being robbed while accessing money, and lack of privacy that would allow them to protect their savings from others.

"Over 80 percent of the small business conducted in the Pacific by women is in little marketplaces," said Dr. Sharman Stone, Australia's Ambassador for Women. "When they only had cash it was extremely dangerous for them to get that cash home, and to retain that cash once they got home."[17] With Bitcoin and cryptocurrencies, they are physically safer, can circumvent inflation and hold their own money.

> Women are the majority of Kenya's population; they perform 70% of the agricultural labor, but they own less than 1% of the land and control very little of the income produced by their labor.[18]

56% of all unbanked adults globally are women. Women are overrepresented among the unbanked in most economies. This is true even in economies that have successfully increased account ownership and have a relatively small share of adults who are unbanked.[19] In the United States, Middle East and North Africa two-thirds of the unbanked are women.[20]

A study in Kenya found that access to mobile money services delivered big benefits, especially for women. It enabled women-headed

---

17   BNY Mellon Supports Global Push for Financial Gender Equality, https://www.bnymellon.com/us/en/about-us/newsroom/company-news/bny_mellon_supports_a_global_push_for_financial_gender_equality.html

18   Georgetown Journal of International Law, https://www.law.georgetown.edu/international-law-journal/wp-content/uploads/sites/21/2018/08/4-Kenya-Report-508.pdf

19   World Bank, Global ID Coverage, Barriers, and Use by the Numbers : An In-Depth Look at the 2017 ID4D-Findex Survey, https://globalfindex.worldbank.org/sites/globalfindex/files/chapters/2017%20Findex%20full%20report_chapter2.pdf

20   World Bank, The Little Data Book on Financial Inclusion 2018, https://openknowledge.worldbank.org/bitstream/handle/10986/29654/LDB-FinInclusion2018.pdf

households to increase their savings by more than one fifth, allowed 185,000 women to leave farming and develop business or retail activities and helped reduce extreme poverty among women-headed households by 22 percent.

Mobile money services like M-Pesa in Kenya or EcoCash in Zimbabwe have increased access to financial instruments. The problem: these are services by centralized, private companies. The government can interfere, transactions can be censored or accounts can be closed. As an example, in July 2020 the Zimbabwean government blocked pay-outs from EcoCash mobile money accounts to bank accounts or cash.

Financial services can also help people accumulate savings and increase spending on necessities. After being provided with savings accounts, market vendors in Kenya, primarily women, saved at a higher rate and invested 60 percent more in their businesses. Women-headed households in Nepal spent 15 percent more on nutritious foods (meat and fish) and 20 percent more on education after receiving free savings accounts. Moreover, farmers in Malawi who had their earnings deposited into savings accounts spent 13 percent more on farming equipment and increased their crop values by 15 percent.[21]

Bitcoin can lower the cost of receiving payments, leaving people with more of their money. While traditional financial instruments require an ID and proof of address, using Bitcoin is open to everyone. Therefore, Bitcoin can support women in gaining more freedom and self-sovereignty.

For more insights about the living conditions of people in Zimbabwe and their real-life use of Bitcoin in Venezuela, Argentina, Afghanistan,

21 World Bank, The Global Findex Database Measuring Financial Inclusion and the Fintech Revolution 2017, https://www. notion.so/Financial-Inclusion-feb3e3913cb042b9bc0ef525ad0f8272#f24c9e8d868e49fe9052c6lead55e080

Nigeria, and more, listen to my podcast interviews (https://anita.link/show). Regarding the advantages for women using Bitcoin, look up the section "Women in Bitcoin".

3.2.3 Slow, But Safe

One criticism of Bitcoin is that its development is slow and clunky. In fact, reality shows that Bitcoin is the longest standing and technically safest blockchain. It has never been hacked or altered. The reason for this is a community of independent, open-source developers whose first interest is to contribute to the broader social good. Listen to Adam Back (https://anita.link/12), Gloria Zhao (https://anita.link/82), Tim Akinbo (https://anita.link/63), Amiti Uttawar (https://anita.link/62) or Matt Corrallo (https://anita.link/19) to understand how thoughtful and driven they are by their mission. Secondly, the pace of development is deliberately slow. The Silicon Valley mantra of "Move fast and break things" is the opposite of what you want for a 600 billion USD digital asset that is, at the same time, live software.

3.2.4 Internet of Things

An internet native money like bitcoin can be used by machines too. Self-driving electric cars like auto-taxis will be able to recharge themselves at charging stations and pay automatically with bitcoin. This is not science fiction, this is the near future. Andy Schroder from Kentucky is loading his Tesla with real-time machine to machine micropayments over the Bitcoin Lightning Network (http://andyschroder.com/DistributedCharge/) already. This will not be the only innovation that will come from the intersections of new technology, money and communication.

3.2.5 Bitcoin, the Life-Boat

As I laid out in chapter I, it's not a question of whether the current financial system will fall, but when. Even before the COVID-19 pandemic spread globally in spring 2020, nations were in deep debt; the devastating effects were evident in the global and regional wealth gaps. For many years experts have warned the public about it. Simon Dixon had already called out the Great Depression of the 2020s in 2011. Nomi Prins explained the central banks' collusion in her 2018 book of the same name. Satoshi Nakamoto referred to the dangers of a monetary system built on debt and the financial crisis in the white paper.

Bitcoin is debt-free money. One does not simply inflate the supply. It's the perfect alternative to opt-out of the fiat system. In order to hedge against this looming crisis, it makes sense to distribute investments among different assets and thus reduce systemic risk. Gold, equities, bonds, real estate, watches and vintage cars are well-known value protection assets. Bitcoin is a digital value protection asset.

When CEOs of publicly traded companies like Elon Musk and Michael Saylor began to exchange USD cash holdings for bitcoin, they secured their place on the Bitcoin life-boat. Bitcoin was made for individuals. For people like you and me. Now is your chance to exit the sinking boat of fiat currencies. It's not too late, you're still early.

3.2.6 Bitcoin Is Common Good

The Bitcoin network is a public infrastructure; it is a decentralized communications network that is still being built right in front of our eyes. We as individuals could not participate financially, directly from the build out of the internet. Most of us did not own shares of Apple, Google or Facebook. Many hurdles exclude billions of people from investing in start-ups. Bitcoin is open for everyone to invest in its infrastructure. You can also use houses to imagine Bitcoin being digital property: there are only 21 million houses and you can buy a fraction of a house, right down to a door handle.

3.2.7 Bitcoin Encourages Saving

Bitcoin is ideal for long-term saving. If you believe that the value is going to rise in the future, you are encouraged to hold and not to spend your bitcoin on things that are not really necessary.

3.2.8 You Can Afford Bitcoin

You don't have to buy a whole bitcoin. A bitcoin is divisible to a hundred million units. The smallest unit is called a "Satoshi" – after the pseudonymous founding figure, Satoshi Nakamoto. You can buy parts of a bitcoin and start with as little as 20 euros, for example.

3.2.9 Bitcoin and the Functions of Money

Many textbook economists are insisting on the fact that Bitcoin is not money because it does not fulfill the three functional criteria that money must have. These functions were defined by William Stanley Jevons'[22] in 1875, his analysis becoming widely popular in macroeconomic textbooks ever since.

---

22 https://en.wikipedia.org/wiki/William_Stanley_Jevons "William Stanley Jevons"

According to Jevons, Bitcoin is only money if it fulfills these functions:

1. Store of value – the value must remain stable over time
2. Medium of exchange – it is widely accepted in exchange for goods and services
3. Medium of account – it is used as a measure for prices, costs and profits

Source: https://en.wikipedia.org/wiki/Money

1. Store of Value

Critics say bitcoin is not a store of value due to its volatility and potential for short-term losses. Well, as I laid out in chapter 3.1, in the long-term that is not really the case. Further, I question the definition of "stable over time". What is the time frame? Inflation in fiat money in Austria has been 20% over the last decade. All other fiat currencies like the Euro are similarly unreliable stores of value for this very reason.

2. Medium of Exchange

You can use bitcoin as a medium of exchange if you want to. Yes, there is only a small number of companies, services and restaurants that accept bitcoin as payment at the time of writing. But, to do this, you could use different tools and services that you can fill with bitcoin and spend in fiat. On top of that, there are a lot of companies inside the space that already accept and pay wages in bitcoin too.

3. Medium of Account

Fiat money is required to be the medium of account by law. We simply do not have a choice. Bitcoin is based on voluntary use, it is opt-in; if we speculate that the value is going up, we won't spend it. Since the volatility of bitcoin becomes less over time, one day value will hit a plateau and people will start spending bitcoin. Even earlier than this, more and more businesses will start to accept bitcoin, since they will trust that it does not lose value but rather appreciates.

A new form of money that is not forced upon us, but is an opt-in, has to go through certain stages in that order: first, it has to become a store of value, then trust has to be built, then people will use it as a medium of exchange. Only then will be used as a medium of account.

Dismissing Bitcoin because it does not yet fulfill all the functions of money is missing the point.

3.2.10 Comparing the Traits of Money

In 2014 Ryan Walker took the concepts of Darwin's theory of natural selection to compare the evolution of the different forms of money. The table below displays the degree to which gold, fiat and bitcoin fulfill the traditionally recognized traits of money (row 1–8). Government issued measures the degree of centralization and control by authorities (row 9).

> "The arrival of cryptographic-based currencies has enabled key new traits previously not possible with traditional forms of money. Furthermore, the realization of such traits will likely have a dramatic impact on the environment in which these currencies compete. Row 10 and 11 include the specie of cryptocurrency when rated against the traditional and newly realized traits of money." – RYAN WALKER

Traits of Money	Gold	FIAT € | $	Bitcoin
Fungible (interchangeable)	High	High	High
Non-consumable	High	High	High
Portability	Moderate	High	High
Durable	High	Moderate	High
Highly divisible	Moderate	Moderate	High
Secure (cannot be counterfeited)	Moderate	Moderate	High
Easily transactable	Low	High	High
Scarce (predictable supply)	Moderate	Low	High
Government issued	Low	High	Low
Decentralized	Low	Low	High
Programmable	Low	Low	High

The traits of money[23]

Source: Ryan Walker, https://www.coindesk.com/origins-money-darwin-evolution-cryptocurrency

This shows the degree to which gold, fiat, and cryptographic currencies fulfill the traditionally recognized traits of currency as well as the new traits made possible by the discovery of Bitcoin.

As you can see, Bitcoin goes beyond the traditional framework of what money is. It's evolving into a completely new dimension of what money can do and from which applications will be built upon in the future.

---

23 Ryan Walker, https://www.coindesk.com/origins-money-darwin-evolution-cryptocurrency

3.3 Strategic Notes

3.3.1 Words of Warning

Before you get into buying Bitcoin, please read these important notes:

This guide covers the first Bitcoin blockchain, created by Satoshi Nakamoto in 2009, which operates under the acronym BTC or XBT on exchanges. For information about Bitcoin (BTC), see https://bitcoin. org. On http://bitcoin.com, on the other hand, you reach the website of Bitcoin Cash (BCH), which is a split off from 2017.

Be aware that there are many spin-offs of the original Bitcoin. They have names like Bitcoin Cash (BCH), Bitcoin SV (BSV), Bitcoin Gold (BTG), Bitcoin Diamond (BCD) or Bitcoin 2 (BTC2). These are not "cheaper" bitcoin, but independent, different assets. They use the same name as Bitcoin to benefit from its notoriety, but do not maintain the same strengths or popularity as the real Bitcoin (BTC).

Bitcoin is a common good, without trademark rights. If you were to start a company today and call it "Apple Premium", you would receive a lawsuit for trademark infringement from Apple very quickly. This does not apply to Bitcoin because it is open source, which promotes innovation and inclusion. In the case of naming a spin-off something like Bitcoin Cash, it is confusing and should be avoided.

The use of Bitcoin is legal in most countries of the world, but a state ban could come into force at any time, theoretically preventing the use of Bitcoin by individuals. In any case, a ban could result in a loss of value and switching your bitcoin back into fiat currencies could be

difficult. Since the core Bitcoin community are highly committed users, even if your country bans bitcoin, you will always find someone who will happily exchange your bitcoin for fiat.

The price of bitcoin is determined by supply and demand. It is possible at any time – and has also happened several times – that the price drops sharply in a short time and you cannot withdraw or exchange your bitcoin as quickly as desired.

Use only as much money as you can lose without getting into financial problems. You are responsible for the safe custody of your capital. In case of loss or theft, there is no recovery option.

In addition to bitcoin, there are more than 4,000 other crypto assets to date, all of which have different objectives and uses. Learn more about the intentions, the team and the technology behind it before you invest, if at all.

The emergence of these other assets can affect the price of bitcoin. Another currency could become the leading digital currency, although currently most of the acceptance and growth is within Bitcoin (BTC).

Don't get carried away with quick promotions because someone is giving you a "get rich quick" offer and promises to buy and manage coins for you. Unfortunately, many people play nasty games and stage multi-level marketing offers, or Ponzi schemes (https://anita.link/ponzi).

If someone asks you to "join" Bitcoin or is writing "BitCoin", be aware. You don't need to join anything to use Bitcoin, there is no need to buy an entry package or anything like that – these are most likely scams.

If you are waiting to buy a Bitcoin ETF, you won't own bitcoin and won't use bitcoin. You will only be exposed to the price action. You only own and control your bitcoin if you manage your private keys yourself. You can find out how to do this on the following pages.

3.3.2 Privacy in the Digital Age

Bitcoin is pseudonymous. This means that your wallet and your Bitcoin addresses are not linked to your identity as neither your name, place of residence nor IP address is stored.

An exception to this is to create a user account on a centralized Bitcoin exchange when you exchange fiat for bitcoin. Here, as with traditional banks, proof of identity and registration can be required. In certain circumstances, tax offices and government agencies can force an exchange to release your identifying data and related Bitcoin addresses.

If you publish your Bitcoin address on the internet or announce it anywhere else, everyone can check how many coins you own in a block explorer. Be careful with this and don't always use the same Bitcoin address. The wallets that I'll present to you later will automatically create many different Bitcoin addresses so you don't have to worry about that.

Bitcoin is not as anonymous as it is often assumed. All cash flows can be analyzed with sufficient effort. Companies such as Chainalysis specialize in these big data evaluations and clients, such as banks, can pay for this service. Work is underway to improve the privacy of Bitcoin. Over the next two years, there will be innovations here that do not interfere with the use of Bitcoin and offer more data protection.

The cryptocurrency Monero, which has been in existence since 2014, offers already built-in privacy protection. Here the addresses are not publicly visible and blockchain analysis is not possible.

3.4 How Do I Get Bitcoin?

You can acquire bitcoin in three ways:

- you exchange fiat for it
- you earn it
- you mine it

The first option is the one most of us choose. You can use an online exchange or a Bitcoin ATM and sell your fiat money for bitcoin.

Earning it is the better option. You could free up your basement and sell goods for bitcoin, or work as a freelancer and get paid in bitcoin et cetera.

Mining is not an option for most private households anymore. In the early days of Bitcoin, it was possible to mine on your computer. Today, sophisticated hardware – ASICs miners – is required and you need a very cheap source of electricity to remain profitable.

In the next chapters we will go into the requirements to hold and use Bitcoin.

4 STAIRCASE OF FINANCIAL SOVRYNTY

"Not your keys, not your coins." – ANDREAS M. ANTONOPOULOS

As you have read in the previous chapters, Bitcoin's primary strength is its uncensorability, which gives you financial sovereignty. That is – besides the fixed 21 million supply – the main differentiator to all other forms of money. It protects you from bail-ins like in Cyprus in 2014 and from inflation devaluing your funds. It ends the enforced financialization of your money through banking and financial products. It gives you full control over your funds, enables you to move globally while bringing your money with you. It's an alternative, an opt-out of the fiat system – all you need are 12 English words: your seed phrase.

> "Bitcoin is uncensorable and non-inflatable. These are its most important properties." – ANITA POSCH

If you do not have those seed phrase words, you do not have the privileges and the freedom stated above.

4.1 Risks of Custodial Wallets

It's important to note that there is a big difference between custodial wallets and non-custodial wallets. You only get control of the seed phrase when you use a non-custodial (self-hosted) wallet. Exchanges like Coinbase, Kraken, Binance, Bitpanda, etc., do not give you the private keys to your own wallets. While it might be more convenient to hold bitcoin in a wallet on a centralized exchange, it's no different to a bank. You do not own the bitcoin in your exchange account, which can be a big problem if the exchange gets hacked, something which has already happened many times. For instance, I remind you of Mt. Gox, the biggest hack to date that happened in 2014. No day goes by without cases of frozen accounts, or flagging of tainted coins and, sometimes, the regulatory halting of trading. As well as that, those exchanges need you to register and fulfill all KYC identification requirements (know-your-customer and anti-money laundering regulations), which is a hurdle for billions of people, excluding them from banking and now from using crypto exchanges too. On top of that, these KYC regulations are intruding on your privacy. Luckily, Bitcoin is built for everyone. To mitigate the counter-party risks of custodial wallets you should skip these exchanges and use a non-custodial wallet from the start.

> "This illusion that money in the bank is safer than money under the mattress is very much a position of privilege." – ANDREAS M. ANTONOPOULOS

For people outside of the "western developed world", there is no such thing as a secure bank account. This is a privilege. You might think you would rather leave your money on the exchange because you don't want to have the hassle and responsibility of holding your own money.

You can do that, but it's not what Satoshi Nakamoto intended and it makes you vulnerable.

Once you have learned and executed the steps to financial freedom, you will see that it is not as difficult as it may first seem.

4.2 3 Steps to Financial Sovereignty

"With great freedom, comes great responsibility." – DR. STEPHANIE MURPHY

Stephanie Murphy, co-host of the "Speaking of Bitcoin" podcast, frames the financial freedom model as a staircase with different levels of sovereignty. Since Bitcoin is a technology in development, the grade of freedom that one can reach is changing all the time. This book will give you guidance to reach step 2: the "Your keys, your coins" level. Reaching the "Don't trust, verify" level will become much easier in the coming years. At the moment it requires technical know-how and a greater effort in time and resources, but in principle everyone can reach it.

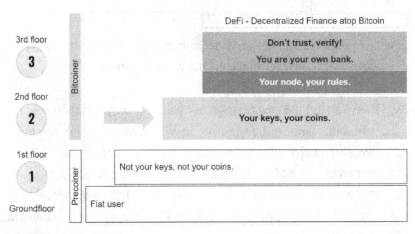

3 steps to financial sovereignty
Source: Anita Posch

GROUNDFLOOR You are a pre-coiner – since you are reading my book you must be interested in Bitcoin, but you do not own any.

IST FLOOR You are getting to know BTC with a custodial solution on a centralized exchange, but you don't control any of the keys. You have some independence because you're invested in a cryptocurrency and not solely fiat anymore. But it's not a lot of independence because you rely on a third party, which comes with the counter-party risks mentioned above. You are on the **"not your keys, not your coins"** level.

Ideally, you skip the first floor and go to the 2nd floor as fast as possible.

2ND FLOOR You take control of your keys and store them yourself securely on a non-custodial wallet that gives you your seed. This is a much higher degree of financial sovereignty. You can do that with a mobile wallet on your smartphone for small amounts or – the best way and highly recommended – with a hardware wallet for larger amounts. You reach the **"your keys, your coins"** level. You have reached a very high level of independence.

From here on the steps are for experienced users. They give you even more sovereignty, privacy and control over your bitcoin.

3RD FLOOR You get full sovereignty over your funds by connecting your hardware wallet with your own full node. With this setup, you can not only view and receive information about your transactions but also verify mined blocks and transactions without relying on 3rd parties. You don't have to trust anyone else anymore and have a high level of privacy and control. **"You are your own bank"** and have now reached the **"Don't trust, verify"** level.

You can take these security and independence measures even further with air-gapped solutions, multi-sig setups and more.

On top of that staircase, decentralized financial solutions like bitcoin borrowing and lending are emerging.

Ultimately, if all you want to do is hedge against inflation and use Bitcoin as a store of value, **reaching the 2nd floor, "your keys, your coins" is the goal**. I will show you how to reach this level of sovereignty in the next chapters.

4.3 Securing Your Funds

As mentioned in the previous chapter, our goal is to reach the "Your keys, your coins" level.

To buy, use and store bitcoin, you will need:

- Bitcoin wallet = your digital money deposit box. A more precise analogy is a digital key-chain for your moneyboxes.
- Bitcoin addresses = one or more unique addresses for your funds on the blockchain, your receiving addresses (more precisely an unspent transaction output UTXO)
- Seed = the recovery data for your Bitcoin wallet.

4.3.1 Bitcoin Wallet

Think of a wallet like a public lock-box with multiple sections. Anyone can deposit money in each of the sections. Only the owner of the private keys can unlock a section and move the money it holds. Your

Bitcoin wallet consists of all the sections and holds all the private keys to unlock them. Private keys and Bitcoin addresses are generated from the seed. The seed is the root of all keys and addresses. It's like a bucket in which all your private keys are stored.

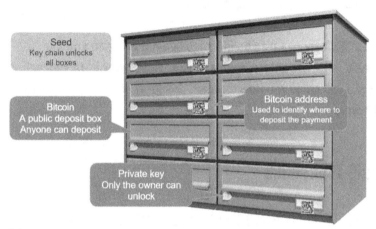

Defining terms

Source: Anita Posch, inspired by Andreas M. Antonopoulos

The wallet is an app on your phone or software on your computer, which handles everything in the background – your private keys, your addresses, and sending and receiving bitcoin.

Bitcoin wallets contain keys, not coins. Each user has a wallet containing keys. Wallets are really just key-chains containing pairs of private/public keys. Your funds are recorded on the Bitcoin blockchain.

4.3.2 Bitcoin Address

To receive bitcoin, you need a Bitcoin address to which someone can send you bitcoin. The Bitcoin address consists of a long series of digits and letters.

An example of a Bitcoin address:
346n4apJCQPg2XAXU3bfNQTogz4PyTkrEf

Typing 34 digits is of course very impractical, therefore QR codes of the addresses are commonly used and are usually created automatically by your wallet.

BTC address as QR code

Bitcoin is pseudonymous, meaning there is no requirement for you to connect your email address or personal identification with a wallet. However, the Bitcoin blockchain is transparent, which means that your Bitcoin addresses are publicly viewable on the internet. For example, you can search for it at Blockcypher and see all current transactions and values. Here is an example link: https://anita.link/explorer

Therefore, for privacy reasons, do not share your Bitcoin addresses in connection with your identity on the internet. Privacy is also the reason why you should not re-use addresses. Most Bitcoin wallets automatically provide you with fresh addresses for each transaction.

Let's get to the most important part of securing your bitcoin: the seed.

4.3.3 Seed and Private Keys

Since the seed is the root of all private keys, no one else must have access to it. The person who knows the seed has ultimate control over the funds.

The seed (sometimes called mnemonic phrase or backup phrase) is a sequence of 12 or 24 English words that gives you access to the private keys of your wallet addresses, and therefore access to your coins. This means that this order of words must remain secret. Anyone who knows the seed can access and take over your coins. Why?

Your coins are not inside your digital wallet as they are inside your regular physical wallet. Instead, they are recorded on the blockchain. Compare this to an email and a letter. You can access your email account from anywhere in the world because your emails are stored online, while your letterbox is stationary. This applies similarly to Bitcoin.

Worldwide access to your assets is always possible with the seed, regardless of your wallet manufacturer. When selecting your wallet, look out for the term "HD wallet" (Hierarchical Deterministic). HD wallets allow you to switch to another manufacturer's HD wallet, take the seed and restore your coins.

Suppose your smartphone gets corrupted, you can't access your Bitcoin wallet app anymore and need to switch to a new phone. You install a fresh version of your Bitcoin wallet and import the seed from your first wallet. Access to your funds is restored.

The seed is generated by the wallet app during the initial setup. Most wallets guide you through the setup and instruct you to write down the seed words on a sheet of paper. If your wallet doesn't offer it right away, look for the "Create Backup" or "Backup" feature and follow the steps. The creation of the seed works in the opposite way to the creation of a password as you commonly know it on websites. It is not you who determines the password, but the wallet itself.

The order of words is IMPORTANT! You must write down the words exactly in the order in which they appear.

> Example seed: cruise item paper slim vocal power like video snap museum mirror sun

Write the seed by hand on a piece of paper and store it safely. Do not take a screenshot, do not store it on your phone or computer that is connected to the internet as all those places can get hacked. There is more information about security in chapter 5.

Since your funds are not inside your wallet but stored on the blockchain, you can move globally and take your bitcoin funds wherever you go. You just need to remember the 12-24 seed words in the correct order. After passing customs without a mobile phone, you get yourself a new wallet and import the seed. Magic.

4.4 Wallet Types

There are different types of wallets depending on the device, security requirements and supported cryptocurrencies. To decide which wallet is best for you I will provide some thoughts and industry standards as guidance. Ultimately, you have to decide which wallet is the best for you. Since Bitcoin is such a novel technology, wallet software is changing constantly. You need to consider that you will need to do upgrades and sometimes change the wallet manufacturer because of

new functionalities; there are constantly new wallets on the market. This should not turn you off, I just want to make you aware of it. In the last few years, I used more and more wallets to test them or to be able to use new functionalities. Therefore I will recommend wallets that I have used myself and that have a very good reputation among industry experts.

4.4.1 Wallet Security

The better protected a wallet's software is from outside attacks over the internet, the more secure it is. Therefore, the basic categorization is between hot storage and cold storage solutions. Hot wallets, like mobile wallets and desktop wallets, are apps that connect to the internet and are therefore at risk from hackers, viruses or regulatory and counter-party risks. Cold storage solutions like hardware wallets are not always-online and therefore are much more secure.

Additionally, your smartphone, whether Android or iOS, is more secure than your laptop or PC. Desktop Windows systems are less secure than Apple devices at the time of writing. Within the different smartphone operating systems, there are fewer differences in the level of security.

On top of these considerations, you need to use a wallet that supports your favorite cryptocurrencies. Since this is a BTC guide, I suggest you use a bitcoin-only wallet. The more cryptocurrencies a software such as a wallet app has to handle, the more complex the development and maintenance of the software is from the manufacturer's end. More complexity brings higher risks of bugs and vulnerabilities.

In the years since Bitcoin's release, using a hardware wallet has proven to be the best way to store your private keys. A hardware wallet is a small device that stores private keys offline, similar to a USB stick.

Hardware wallets require maintenance and a computer or smartphone. If you don't want to worry about software updates, or do not own such a device, you can use the Card Wallet as a cold storage alternative. It is a product by the oldest Austrian bitcoin broker Coinfinity and the Austrian State Printing House.

4.4.2 Industry Standards

In each case, you need to trust the wallet manufacturers to a higher or lesser degree. The **industry's preferred and recommended cold storage solutions are hardware wallets**.

Depending on the amount your wallet has to manage, it is standard to use a combination of **a smartphone wallet for small amounts that you want to have with you on the go** and **hardware wallets for large amounts like savings in your bank account**.

If your bitcoin funds reach an amount that you would rather have secured to an even higher degree, then you should look for multi-signature solutions. But be aware: Multi-sig solutions are **not for beginners**! You really need to know what you are doing.

As an alternative, you can use a company called Casa and their industry-leading multi-sig solutions. Or you can get several hardware wallets to split your funds onto more devices, which lowers the risk of device or manufacturer flaws.

4.5 Wallet Recommendations Overview

4.5.1 Hot Storage

Mobile Wallets

For iOS and Android
- Blockstream Green (Bitcoin, Liquid) (https://blockstream.com/green/)
- Hexa wallet (https://hexawallet.io/)

If you want to use Bitcoin and micro-payments on the Lightning Network:
- Muun Wallet (https://muun.com/)
- Breez Wallet (https://breez.technology/)
- Electrum (https://electrum.org)

Desktop Wallets

Because of the security risks stated above, I don't use software wallets on my computer, except for when I use them in combination with hardware wallets. For this, I use Electrum or the hardware manufacturer's native software.

- Blockstream Green (Bitcoin, Liquid) (https://blockstream.com/green/)
- Blue Wallet (Bitcoin non-custodial and Lightning custodial) (https://bluewallet.io/)
- Electrum (Bitcoin and Lightning, for more tech-savvy users) (https://electrum.org)

4.5.2 Cold Storage

Hardware Wallets

Hardware wallets manage your coins, bitcoin addresses and associated private keys without them ever "touching" the internet. Even if your device is virus-contaminated or has been hacked, your funds are safe and you can send and receive payments. You need to manually confirm transactions on these external devices – this ensures that no intruder on your computer can take over your funds.

The following manufacturers and devices have recently established themselves in the hardware wallet market. SatoshiLabs from Prague has been producing hardware wallets since 2012. The company Ledger from Paris was founded in 2014. SHIFT Cryptosecurity from Zurich has been on the market since 2015 and Canadian company Coinkite has been in the Bitcoin space since 2012.

- BitBox02 bitcoin-only edition https://anita.link/bitbox02 (my readers get 5 % off) – SHIFT Cryptosecurity
- Trezor One, Model T https://anita.link/trezor – SatoshiLabs
- Ledger Nano S, Nano X https://anita.link/ledger – Ledger
- Coldcard (for tech-savvy users) https://anita.link/coldcard – Coinkite

The Coldcard is different to the other models because it is an air-gapped device – it can be used without ever being connected to a computer. That's why some people refer to it as cold-cold storage, being even more secure. For novices, I recommend one of the first three company's devices.

Some hardware wallets (none of the above) use Bluetooth as a connection method. I advise against this because Bluetooth technology is considered relatively unsafe. It is better to connect the hardware wallet with the supplied USB cable.

Never buy a hardware wallet from strangers on eBay or Amazon, and, of course, don't buy it second hand. Always purchase it directly from the manufacturer's website, the manufacturer's Amazon page or a dealer you trust. Make sure that the device is sealed as stated on the manufacturer's website. Most of the recommended devices above have tamper-evident packaging to make sure that the device is used for the first time and has not been manipulated. Ledger deliberately chooses not to use anti-tamper seals on its packaging because they can potentially be counterfeited. Genuine Ledger devices contain a secure chip that prevents physical tampering and allows users to verify the software and hardware integrity using Ledger's guides. In any case, no manufacturer is sending the seed with the device!

In addition to the device, the vendor provides wallet software to manage your coins. For privacy reasons, many users take the vendor wallet only to do the initialization and backup of the device (write down the seed) and for firmware updates. After that, they use a wallet like Electrum for managing the coins.

Offline wallets

Paper Wallet

On the internet, you will find recommendations for using paper wallets. They are self-generated bitcoin addresses with their private and public keys that you can print out on paper. Since you generate and print them out yourself, you do not have to spend money on them. But, they are difficult to generate securely. The security measures that you need to take are extremely high. **I advise against using them**.

Really, if you do not want to pay the 50–100 USD required to buy a hardware wallet to secure higher amounts than you carry around comfortably on your phone, then you should reconsider using bitcoin as a store of value in the first place.

If you simply cannot afford a hardware wallet, use your phone in the meantime. As soon as you have saved enough funds, get yourself a hardware wallet.

Card Wallet

The Card Wallet (product) is in principle a paper wallet, but it is produced by professionals with high security standards. However, you need to trust the manufacturers to not record the private keys to the card. You can use the Card Wallet as an alternative if you do not own a computer or smartphone or do not want to take care of the maintenance of your hardware wallet. https://cardwallet.com/anita (my readers get 20% off)

The industry's preferred and **recommended cold storage solution is a hardware wallet**.

5.1 Safety Measures

All databases can get hacked. Search your email on https://haveibeenpwned.com/ – if you're lucky you have not been pwned, but billions of other accounts have. Therefore, it is important to follow general security measures that apply even more while using Bitcoin.

5.1.1 Hardware and Software Setup

You can use popular browsers such as Firefox, Opera, Brave or Chrome. Browser extensions that block Javascript and Cookies are recommended. Ghostery, NoScript and ScriptSafe are the kind of extensions you can add to your browser. "HTTPS everywhere" enforces an SSL connection to all websites, including those that do not yet offer SSL.

Be aware that some online stores do not work properly with those extensions turned on, so you have to disable them manually.

It is important that you keep your devices safe.

5.1.2 Updates

This advice applies to all your devices: perform all suggested software updates. For your computer's operating system as well as for your smartphone. Always use the latest version of your wallet and firmware software on your hardware wallet.

5.1.3 Email Addresses

Do not use one email address for everything. Get yourself disposable email addresses that you only use one time. You can also buy a domain that you only use for fake email addresses that you forward to your main address.

5.1.4 Secure Passwords

Use secure passwords for all online services. Your birthday, place of residence, the name of your cat or 1234567 are not secure passwords. Whole sentences with digits, spaces, upper and lower case letters and special characters are strong passwords.

Use a different password for each website on which you log in. Otherwise, a hacker with only one password can enter all the services you are registered with. Do not store these passwords in a Word file or anything like that on your computer. A Word document is easy for hackers to steal and read.

You can use software like 1Password, Bitwarden or KeePass (free and open source). These are encrypted password databases, where you can generate and store all your passwords and you only need to remember one password to open it.

5.1.5 PIN

Set up a PIN for your wallet software so that no one can easily open your wallet on your device.

5.1.6 2FA

Use a 2 factor authentication method to secure your accounts. Do not use SMS/text as the 2 factor authentication method because of SIM swapping attacks. Instead, install an authenticator app like and OTP or TOTP on your phone.

5.1.7 SIM Swapping

SIM swapping is when someone hijacks your SIM and telephone number. They can then use your phone number to login to all connected accounts where you activated 2 factor authentication with text/SMS. SIM swapping is an attack to get into your primary email account. If the attackers can access the primary email account that is associated with 2FA to your phone number, they can find all the Bitcoin exchange accounts you are using with 2FA and wipe them out.

The attack is often started by calling customer services at your telecom provider (Verizon, Vodafone, AT & T, Magenta,...). They say something along the lines of "I am the owner of the phone number, I lost my phone, please transfer my number to my new SIM". The

customer services person will ask for a piece of personal information to verify your identity. The attackers will then try a lot of tricks. They badger the support person to get small bits of information from them, hang up and call someone else and use that snippet of information to build to the next level. They then get more information and keep building until they have enough information to persuade the last person that they are the account owner and get the SIM transferred.

They will go after all crypto exchanges where you might have set up an account with your email address and phone number.

When they know your email, they will try to change your account password with the "forgot password" functionality. Good sites will not tell them if the account exists. The attackers will try to do a password reset or try to get a text message verification.

What You Can Do – Gmail Example

Lock down your primary email account and remove your phone number from your email account (such as a Gmail account). Here is how it's done: https://anita.link/removegmail. Use a different password for every account on every website or service. As a Gmail user, you can enroll in the Google Advanced Protection Program, which defends against targeted online attacks.

5.2 Phishing Attacks

In 2020, the marketing database of the French hardware manufacturer Ledger was hacked. The devices are safe, but thousands of email addresses, phone numbers and even home addresses of customers were leaked and can be found by anyone on the internet. This is an absolute disaster because there's a high chance that people ordering a hardware wallet own bitcoin too. In the worst case, you will be "visited" at home. Most likely are threats via email and phishing attacks. To prevent this, keep in mind that you may never need to use your physical address for delivery of a Bitcoin related product such as a hardware wallet. You could organize a postbox for yourself. In the US there are services that can receive mail for you (CMRAs). If possible, do not even use your real name when ordering. Get yourself a second phone number and use this in case the vendor requests one. Give them a disposable email address that you only use for this specific order.

Phishing attacks are attempts to scare or manipulate you so that you enter your seed words on the attacker's website. For instance, you could receive an email saying: "Your ledger device has been corrupted or deactivated, visit this link and enter your 12 seed words to save your funds," or "We have detected a large withdrawal from your Ledger. You have 24 hours to respond to make this transaction valid. We are sorry, we can not reach your Ledger it seems to be corrupted. We are going to authorize the withdrawal unless you start the recovery process, give us your 24 seed words," or "you have received an airdrop. Money is coming into your account, all we need is a verification, please start your recovery process and give us your 24 seed words."

The attackers try to make you act fast without thinking. If you receive such a mail. Stop. Do not do anything. Because no one can seize your money, no one can remotely disable your hardware wallet. That is the whole point of a decentralized currency like bitcoin.

Never trust email! Especially: never click on the links attached.

Bookmark the real websites of official sites of Ledger, Shift Crypto, Trezor etc. or type the domain name yourself in the browser address bar

 (L)EARN BITCOIN

Ledger <support@ledger.eu>
to h • • • • • • • • • •   Show details

Ledger Logo

Dear Customer,

This is an automated email to inform you that

24-Word Seed Recovery to Electrum is Initiated.

Please note that it can take up to 24 hours to deliver all the funds to your new wallet. After that your funds cannot be accessed by Ledger hardware wallet anymore.

If it wasn't you, report your recovery phrase immediately so our team can freeze the process in time. Otherwise just ignore this email.

Phishing mail

Source: Anita Posch

and look up the SSL authentication certificate. The attackers will send you to a fake website that looks the same as the real one. The only difference is the URL. One of the new tricks is to use domains with Unicode characters that look the same as the real domain. For instance, can you notice the stain underneath the l of electrum? If you open that URL you see electrum.org, but are visiting xn--eectrum-9hb.org instead.

ⓘ 🔒 https://electrum.org		ⓘ 🔒 https://xn--eectrum-9hb.org

← → C ⌂	🦊 Firefox	about:config		
Search: 🔍 punycode				
Preference Name	⌃	Status	Type	Value
network.IDN_show_punycode		modified	boolean	true

Source: @ElectrumWallet, https://twitter.com/ElectrumWallet/status/1446786045231472657s=20

Browsers like Opera and Chrome will warn you, but Firefox doesn't do this by default. You can change that by enabling "punycode" in Firefox, see https://anita.link/puny.

5.3 3-2-1 Rule for Storing Your Seed

The seed consists of 12–24 English words. Nowadays, more wallets use 12 words instead of 24 because they provide a high enough level of security and are easier to remember and store.

Write the seed on a piece of paper by hand when you first initialize your wallet. Make sure that the order is correct and check the written words multiple times. Note the vendor, model and the wallet software too. You might need this information in case you want to recover your funds.

If you set up a hardware wallet you should send a small amount of bitcoin to it to make sure that everything works. After receiving the small amount, delete the software from the device and restore it with the words you have written down previously. This is an important step that you should not skip.

After that, it is advisable to take the following security measures to prevent you from losing your seed. When people lose access to their funds it's more often because they have lost their seed or made a mistake writing it down and not because their devices have been hacked.

3: Write down the seed three times

2: On at least two different media (laminated paper, engraved or stamped on steel) and store it in a safe place for protection against fire, loss and theft.

1: additionally, store a backup in a different location, preferably at least 100 kilometres away.

Jameson Lopp, one of my podcast guests, is testing steel plates that can be used to secure the seed for the long term. He exposes them to fire and pressure to check longevity. Not all products are made of steel or titanium, which is why they melt in fire. The tests can be found here: https://anita.link/metalseed

Don't get creative! Dividing the words into two or more parts and storing them in different locations is a common mistake. You only need to lose one part and you will no longer be able to access your coins.

- Never give the seed to someone you don't trust with your money!
- Do not enter the seed on any websites or electronic devices!

- The seed is not required to send or receive bitcoin.
- No credible individual or entity would ask for your seed.
- Check the storage locations of your seed words regularly!
- Set up an inheritance plan – worst cases do happen and if you do not instruct your beneficiaries correctly, your bitcoin are lost. I recommend Pamela Morgan's book on Cryptoasset Inheritance Planning https://anita.link/inheritance

5.3.1 Passphrase

A passphrase is an additional way to secure your funds on top of the seed. If you add a passphrase, the software creates an additional wallet that you can use to protect yourself from physical attacks. If someone gets hold of your seed, they still can not access your funds because they do not have the passphrase.

Example: You might want to leave the minority of your funds in the basic "non-passphrase" wallet and move the majority of your funds to a passphrase-protected wallet. The idea behind this is that if you ever find yourself in a situation where somebody is trying to extort a ransom from you or puts you under duress, you can safely unlock your wallet and only give the attacker access to the normal wallet (which only contains a small amount of funds).

This sounds great, but there are also risks involved.

1. Because the passphrase is not stored anywhere automatically, you need to take **all necessary precautions** in order to make sure that the passphrase stays safe and accessible e.g. by making a physical backup.

2. If the passphrase is lost, you **will not be able to access that wallet** anymore and any coins stored in that wallet will become inaccessible.

With a passphrase, you do not only need to store your seed but the passphrase too. Now you have to find long term secure storage for the seed AND the passphrase, which makes it a more complicated process. Be aware: In order to restore a wallet of this type, you would need your seed AND the passphrase you used for that wallet to restore access to the funds.

Since physical attacks happen rather rarely, storing the seed with the 3-2-I method should be sufficient.

5.3.2 Alternative Backups

Some wallets use different mechanisms for the backup. For instance, the Muun wallet uses a combination of recovery code – that you need to write down like a seed – and an emergency kit.

5.4 Learning by Doing

It can be intimidating to start using Bitcoin because it's real money. That is why it is a good practice to start with very small amounts.

For your first attempts, install a wallet on your phone, search for a Bitcoin ATM https://anita.link/atm close to you or attend a local Bitcoin meet-up and exchange a small amount. Get a wallet for your computer and send bitcoin in between your two wallets to different addresses.

The best time to do this is usually on the weekend when the Mempool is not packed with transactions and the fees are lower.

Use different wallet software, reinstall the wallet seed from wallet A to B, use the seed on different devices. You will feel more and more secure maintaining the skills.

5.4.1 Test Receive Address

Before you send a large amount for the first time, make sure that the address is really from the receiver and perform a small test transaction. Always check the Bitcoin address two or three times before sending the transaction. Compare the first and last digits of the address. Bitcoin that you send to an incorrect address are lost.

5.4.2 Test Your Hardware Wallet

Before you save large amounts on a new hardware wallet, you should check the functionality and the seed.

When you set up the device initially, it creates the seed for you that you write down by hand (additionally the vendor, model and software version). Afterwards, you use the vendor software (or another software such as Electrum) and create the first Bitcoin address in your hardware wallet by clicking on "Receive". Then send a small amount to it from your previously installed smartphone wallet. If the amount on the hardware wallet has arrived as confirmed, the first test was successful.

Also, try sending from your hardware wallet to another wallet. For example, you can send a small amount to your smartphone wallet or another address of your hardware wallet. It doesn't particularly matter. The main thing is that you are testing a payment from the hardware wallet too. To do this you must check the receiving address on the hardware wallet and confirm sending with one or more clicks directly on the hardware wallet. This manual confirmation on the device makes hardware wallets secure as only you can press the buttons and no one can hit the buttons virtually over the internet.

Restore Your Wallet

Then make sure that you have your backup/seed! Afterwards, delete all data on your hardware wallet. Some vendors call it "factory reset", "wipe" or "reset the device". Your wallet is empty. Now restore your funds and wallet with the seed. This is called "Restore from recovery word", "Restore wallet", or "Import seed". Then enter your seed phrase on the hardware device. If everything is correct, the wallet is restored and you can see your previous transactions and balance.

Upgrade Firmware and Software

Don't just lock the device away. You should look for updates to the software or for firmware upgrades at least every 6 months. The crypto space is fast moving and new developments are integrated into wallet software on a regular basis.

5.5 Smartphone Lost? Computer Stolen?

5.5.1 Loss, Theft, or Malfunctioning of Your Device

If your device gets stolen, remember that your bitcoin are still listed on the blockchain under your private key. Since you set an access PIN for the wallet, the thief cannot open it. However, they will still try to find a way to crack your PIN.

You should immediately install a new wallet and import the seed that you kept safe to regain access to your funds (see "restore your wallet"). Then, move the coins from your stolen wallet to a new Bitcoin address in your new wallet as soon as you can, repeating the same security setup procedures for the new wallet.

If your device gets corrupted, you follow the same steps, but there is no need to rush to move the coins. Just restore the software wallet and you're done.

6.1 Price Discovery

There is no one official price for bitcoin. It is determined in real time separately on exchanges like Kraken, Bitstamp, Coinbase, Binance etc. There are sites like CoinMarketCap, CoinGecko and BitcoinAverage https://anita.link/average which show you a global average of the prices of several exchanges. Or you can go directly to the website of one of the exchanges and look it up.

The price – which is the exchange rate – is determined by the activities of buyers and sellers of cryptocurrency who are trading it in real time. More demand, higher price. Less supply, higher price. This is why the halving is an important event. Even if the demand stays the same, the smaller supply will move the price up.

Bitcoin is an open market. The market's function is to discover what the real value of bitcoin is. The current price of any commodity in an open market is the average of the prices that people actually agreed and traded on over the past period of time. Nobody is setting the exchange rate, the price of bitcoin is discovered.

6.2 Different Price in a Region

If you look up the exchange rate for bitcoin in different countries you will find differences between nations. For instance, buying bitcoin in Zimbabwe with local currency will be more expensive than with USD. That is not because bitcoin is more expensive in Zimbabwe, but because the demand for the local currency is lower. You cannot move your Zimbabwe Dollar out of the country; even Zimbabweans prefer USD. So, people need to pay a premium to buy bitcoin when they use a lower valued currency.

6.3 All-Time High Tracker

A nice page to look at to find out the time since the last All-Time High (ATH) is Coingecko https://anita.link/ath

6.4 Bitcoin Calculator

Regarding difficulties in converting satoshi to other currencies, such as the question "How much is 0.05 bitcoin or 10,000 satoshi in my fiat currency?":
Here is an easy to use calculator: https://anita.link/calc
Bitcoin currency converter: http://preev.com

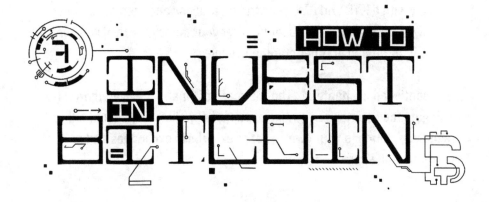

In this chapter, we will explore the different ways you can obtain bitcoin. In general, this is through buying bitcoin by exchanging it for fiat currency or by earning it. The methods differ in the level of self-sovereignty and privacy you can achieve.

7.1 Buying Bitcoin – Custodial

In many cases, people's first interaction with cryptocurrencies is through custodial exchanges like Kraken, Coinbase, Binance, Bitpanda and Bitfinex, just to name a few.

They are called custodial because they possess the keys to your bitcoin. You do get a wallet on these platforms, but it's more like a bank account, leading to counter-party risks such as hacking, seizure or confiscation by governments.

Trading on these exchanges is done off-chain, meaning that transactions are not settled on the blockchain but are only managed inside the platform's databases. This increases the speed of transactions, but at the same time leads to a lack of transparency and security.

To acquire bitcoin in a custodial fashion, you need to open an account, comply with a KYC and AML registration process and then deposit fiat money into the platform's account. After your money's arrival you can trade it for bitcoin or other cryptocurrencies.

As mentioned in chapter 4 "The Staircase of Financial Sovereignty", to mitigate the counter-party risks of custodial wallets you should either send your funds to your own wallet or skip these exchanges and go non-custodial immediately.

7.2 Buying Bitcoin – Non-Custodial

Holding bitcoin in a non-custodial (self-hosted) manner is the desired outcome. It makes your transactions uncensorable and provides maximal freedom over your funds. You can achieve this by buying bitcoin in the right place to begin with.

7.2.1 Bitcoin Broker

A broker is a company that enables you to buy non-custodial bitcoin. Since these are registered companies, they are fully regulated and you need to be identified and go through AML/KYC procedures. Bitcoin brokers will send the amount of bitcoin you bought directly to your Bitcoin address (your wallet, where you hold the seed).

Just to name a few examples of Bitcoin brokers:

- AnyCoin direct (https://anycoindirect.eu/)
- Bity (https://bity.com/)
- Coinfinity (https://coinfinity.co/start-en/)

- Coinnexus (https://coinnexus.ch/en) works without verification up to CHF 1,000 per year.

7.2.2 Peer-to-Peer Purchase in Person

You can visit one of the many Bitcoin meet-ups around the world, connect with fellow Bitcoiners and ask them to sell you some bitcoin for cash. In many countries, people meet in Telegram or Facebook groups to find peers to exchange in person.

7.2.3 Peer-to-Peer Online Purchase

The world's leading P2P exchanges
- LocalBitcoins (https://localbitcoins.com)
- Paxful (https://paxful.com/)

7.2.4 Bitcoin ATMs

A Bitcoin ATM is a machine similar to an ATM, where you can buy bitcoin and other cryptocurrencies with cash. The advantage of Bitcoin ATMs is that you get your bitcoin instantly and in many places, up to a certain threshold, without KYC/AML identification. But be careful as some ATM operators charge above average fees.

- Bitcoin ATM Map (https://bitcoinatmmap.com/)
- Bitrawr ATMs (https://www.bitrawr.com/bitcoin-atms)
- CoinATM Radar (https://coinatmradar.com/)

7.2.5 Bitcoin Gift Cards and Vouchers

In Austria for example, it is possible to buy 'Bitcoinbon' gift cards at petrol stations as well as in kiosks. These gift cards are often found in the display stands where cards for mobile phone credit or Amazon gifts etc. are also sold. You can buy bitcoin gift cards without setting up a wallet and without registration. If you want to convert the value of the cards into coins, you set up a wallet and redeem the coins.

- Azteco (https://azte.co/)
- Bitcoinbon (http://www.bitcoinbon.at/)
- Bitpanda to go (https://www.bitpanda.com/de/togo)
- Coincola (https://www.coincola.com/buy-bitcoin/gift-cards)
- Paxful (https://paxful.com/buy-bitcoin?group=gift-cards&hasScroll=true)

7.3 Non-KYC Bitcoin

7.3.1 KYC/AML

KYC and AML stands for "Know Your Customer" and "Anti-Money Laundering" regulations. Every bank and registered exchange has to comply with these national laws by recording customer information such as:

- Name
- Address
- Phone number
- Drivers license
- Government ID

- A selfie holding a piece of paper with the name of the exchange and the date
- A video call with the exchange

Now, one could argue that we need to find criminals, terrorists, money launderers etc. and therefore these regulations make sense. The problem is that the banks often over-regulate; they demand more data than required and track every single transaction which, in combination with digital money, turns into a surveillance machine worse than George Orwell ever imagined. While we point at and criticize China's central bank digital currency and their overreaching social credit program, we are building similar systems that massively intrude on people's privacy.

KYC / AML has not kept Deutsche Bank, HSBC and many other big players from laundering money, but it prevents billions of people without ID from participating in economical activities. It requires massive bureaucracy, high costs and it puts your privacy at risk because of data leaks. The exchanges know how much you bought, when you bought it, your banking information and the addresses you withdraw to.

With KYC/AML and holding your bitcoin on an exchange, you also break the censorship resistance of Bitcoin. Many exchanges work together with blockchain surveillance companies, which cooperate in many cases directly with the government. Through the Bitcoin blockchain's transparency, any chain analysis company can follow your activity. The exchanges can freeze your account or block your withdrawal.

While I don't think governments will be able to effectively ban Bitcoin from being used – it would be like banning people from thinking, as they only have to remember their seed – they could try to confiscate it,

just as the USA did with gold. If something like this happened, and you have left your money on an exchange – then it's as good as gone.

Executive order 6102, signed on April 5 1933 by US President Franklin D. Roosevelt forbade the hoarding of gold. In 1975, Americans could legally own gold again. Satoshi Nakamoto listed their birthday as April 5, 1975. That's of course no coincidence. It shows Satoshi's intentions, that Bitcoin is about financial freedom.

For more information on how the current financial system is unfair to billions of people around the world, listen to my podcast interview with Zachary Kelman, (https://anita.link/80) an attorney specializing in political, legal, and regulatory issues in and around Bitcoin.

7.3.2 Getting No-KYC Bitcoin

To buy bitcoin without user identification you can:

- earn it
- build something of value and ask for donations
- sell things you don't need anymore
- buy from a friend or at a local meetup
- buy at a Bitcoin ATM
- buy bitcoin gift cards
- go to physical stores where you can buy or sell bitcoin
- use decentralized exchanges like
    - Hodlhodl (https://hodlhodl.com)
    - Bisq (https://bisq.network/)
    - LocalCoinSwap (https://localcoinswap.com/buy-sell/BTC)
    - LocalCryptos (https://localcryptos.com/Bitcoin)
    - Sovryn (https://live.sovryn.app)

Exchange sources: https://kycnot.me/, https://github.com/
cointastical/P2P-Trading-Exchanges/, https://bitcoiner.guide/
nokyconly/

7.4 Costs for Buying Bitcoin

When you buy cryptocurrencies you have to pay fees for the service
provider, just like when you exchange to a foreign currency when you
travel to a different country. The price at which you exchange is
determined by the service provider (see chapter 6). Usually, this is the
market price plus a surcharge for the service. Since each exchange has
its own bitcoin price and different fee structures, there are big
differences in the trading costs between them. You can save money by
comparing trading fees when choosing a specific platform.

There are three points that determine the costs for buying bitcoin, and
each service provider has its own:
- Bitcoin market price
- Trading fees for their service
- Transaction fees, which may be included in the trading fee.

7.5 Wallet Navigator

There are a variety of wallet providers and more are being released
over time. You have to decide whether you want one that is for Bitcoin
only or one for multiple coins. Each wallet offers different
functionalities, security levels and support levels for different sets of
coins. The following questions will help you to choose the basic type of
wallet that will be suited to your needs. You will still need to research
which manufacturer supports which coins.

7.5.1 Step 1 – Select Wallet

Would you like to be able to pay with the wallet on a regular basis?

If you neither use a mobile phone nor computer and do not want to send payments, you can use the Card Wallet. You can send bitcoin or ether to it and save them. As soon as you want to pay it out, you will need to install a wallet. If you do want to make regular payments with it, then a software wallet, possibly in combination with hardware authentication like a Trezor or BitBox02 is more appropriate.

Do you want to keep software and a device up-to-date?

No? Then, again, the Card Wallet is the correct choice for you. You do not have to worry about maintaining a device.

The amount you plan to have on the wallet will be...

Similar to the regular wallet in your pocket: usually a mobile wallet is sufficient. It's free of charge and sufficient for small amounts.
Similar to your bank account: use a hardware wallet. Hardware wallets are highly sought after in Bitcoin bull runs and often sold out (Keep this in mind in your schedule).

There is an extended helper on the Bitcoin.org website (https://bitcoin. org/en/choose-your-wallet), that you can use too. It guides you through the selection based on the operating system (mobile, desktop, hardware wallet) you choose.

7.5.2 Step 2 – Make a Backup of Your Keys

Write down the mnemonic seed – 12 to 24 English words, the name, type and software version of your wallet and store them in a safe place (see chapter 5.3).

7.5.3 Step 3 – Buy Bitcoin

Most wallets include the ability to buy bitcoin directly within their interface. Wallet manufacturers are cooperating with exchanges,

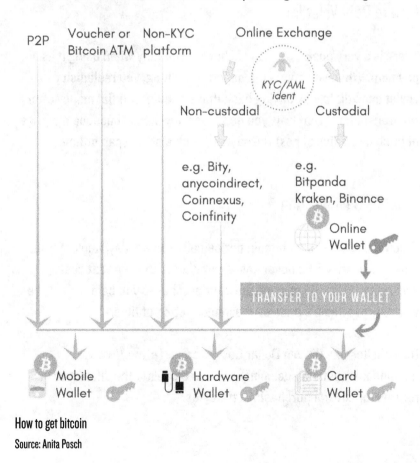

How to get bitcoin

Source: Anita Posch

which in return pay them a commission. If I need to use an exchange I prefer selecting one prior and externally from the wallet. That way I stay independent of the wallet type, can use this one exchange to send bitcoin to all my different wallets, and only have to leave my KYC data in that one exchange, reducing the risk of data breaches. Using non-custodial, non-KYC methods (chapter 7.3) is even better.

7.6 Strategy

7.6.1 How to Defy Volatility

There is a very good way to avoid bitcoin volatility when using it as a payment. When you spend bitcoin on something, you replenish your wallet immediately by buying back those bitcoin with fiat money after the transaction. That way, you don't lose any money because the price of bitcoin remains almost the same in such a short span of time.

7.6.2 Create a Savings Plan

Procure a small sum of bitcoin periodically – every day/week/month. This is also known as dollar cost averaging (DCA) – or fiat cost averaging (FCA). By spacing out your purchases you balance out the volatility of bitcoin's price over a longer period of time.

On websites like Bitcoin Dollar Cost Average (https://www.bitcoindollarcostaverage.com/) you can calculate the differences in returns for several purchasing strategies.

Bitcoin-only FCA services

Austria, Germany: Coinfinity (https://coinfinity.co/sparplan/?ref=6716)
France: StackinSat (https://www.stackinsat.com/)
Europe: Relai (https://relai.ch/)
UK: Coinfloor (https://coinfloor.co.uk/hodl/), xsats (https://xsats.com/)
Australia: Bitaroo (https://support.bitaroo.com.au/hc/en-au/articles/360042838874-Recurring-Buy-DCA-), Amber App (https://amber.app/)
Canada: Bull Bitcoin (https://bullbitcoin.com/)
Nigeria: Bitnob (https://bitnob.com/)
USA: Swan Bitcoin (https://www.swanbitcoin.com/), River (https://river.com/)

7.6.3 Trading

There are countless trading experts online who tell beginners how to "time the market" and predict the movement of bitcoin's price. They try to sell you trading software and seminars. Stop. Don't spend your time and money on trying to do that. You can't time the market. The big players will get you "rekt." On top of that, you will pay a lot of trading fees and keep in mind that you may have to track all trading movements for tax reasons. In some countries your bitcoin gains are tax-free if you do not exchange the coins for 12 months. Each trade can be a new taxable event.

7.6.4 Altcoins

Altcoins is the abbreviation for alternative coins. These are all crypto assets that were created after Bitcoin. Many beginners follow the

advice to "diversify their portfolio" and start to trade their bitcoin with Altcoins. Thousands of Altcoins are listed on Coinmarketcap (https:// coinmarketcap.com/). You can't research all of them and most are not being developed anymore and are worthless. Bitcoin is the first-mover and the asset with the biggest network effect. My personal opinion is, if you want to diversify, do it with your knowledge. Go deeper into the Bitcoin rabbit hole, learn how to self-custody, learn how to set up a node, learn about new developments like DeFi on Bitcoin or learn how to earn bitcoin.

However, you might be tempted to give it a try. Use the website If you had bought crypto (https://ifyouhadboughtcrypto.com/) to compare your earnings in recent years if you had invested in Bitcoin or Ethereum, Dash, Ripple, Cardano, Dogecoin, Litecoin or Bitcoin Cash.

7.6.5 If I Had Only...I'm Too Late

If you had only bought Bitcoin in 2011, you would be very rich by now. That is true and I would congratulate without envy, because you were one of the few people who believed in Bitcoin and were ready to put your hard earned money into a risky experiment. None of the early adopters knew that Bitcoin would rise like it has done. It was very difficult to secure your keys back then and many bitcoin were lost or stolen. If you had made it through and preserved your coins, you might have sold it all in 2014, maybe 2017? It is pointless to ponder about "what if". We are still in the early days. If you are starting to educate yourself and use Bitcoin now, you're still leagues ahead of the masses. It's never too late to learn about Bitcoin.

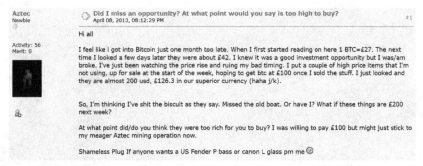

| Aztec
Newbie | Did I miss an opportunity? At what point would you say is too high to buy? | #1 |
| | April 08, 2013, 08:12:29 PM | |

Hi all

Activity: 56
Merit: 0

I feel like i got into Bitcoin just one month too late. When I first started reading on here 1 BTC=£27. The next time I looked a few days later they were about £42. I knew it was a good investment opportunity but I was/am broke. I've just been watching the price rise and ruing my bad timing. I put a couple of high price items that I'm not using, up for sale at the start of the week, hoping to get btc at £100 once I sold the stuff. I just looked and they are almost 200 usd, £126.3 in our superior currency (haha j/k).

So, I'm thinking I've shit the biscuit as they say. Missed the old boat. Or have I? What if these things are £200 next week?

At what point did/do you think they were too rich for you to buy? I was willing to pay £100 but might just stick to my meager Aztec mining operation now.

Shameless Plug If anyone wants a US Fender P bass or canon L glass pm me 😊

Here is someone thinking to be too late in 2013

Source: BitcoinTalk, https://bitcointalk.org/index.php?topic=170725.0

7.6.6 Taxes

I'm not a tax advisor but what I can say is, learn about the regulations and tax requirements in your jurisdiction. The Bitcoin blockchain is transparent and more and more tax authorities will require exchanges to hand them their trading data. Keep proofs of your purchases in case authorities start investigating.

8.1 Transaction Fees

A mining fee has to be paid for every bitcoin transaction and these fees are required for the operation of the Bitcoin network to continue. The work of miners is rewarded with these fees and newly minted bitcoin (see chapter 2.3). Mining is an essential factor in the Bitcoin protocol. After a block of transactions has been mined, it is attached to the blockchain. This is the way to ensure the security of the network. Since Bitcoin has a fixed supply limit of 21 million coins, the miners would no longer receive any remuneration for their performance after reaching this maximum supply, and would no longer be interested in processing transactions and thus maintaining the blockchain. Therefore, Satoshi Nakamoto introduced transaction fees. According to the white paper, the aim is to keep these fees lower than the comparable fees and costs of the traditional banking system. However, it is not the case that transfers are free of charge simply because, in theory, there is no need for intermediaries or banks.

When you're buying bitcoin via an exchange, the transaction fee (mining fee) is usually not adjustable and is fixed by the provider.

In your non-custodial Bitcoin wallet, you can determine the transaction fee for outgoing payments by yourself. The higher you set the fee, the faster your transaction will be processed by the miners because they pick the transactions with the highest fees first. If your transfer is not time-sensitive, you can choose a lower fee.

For more control you can estimate the fee and the confirmation speed on pages like Mempool.space (https://mempool.space/) or Johoe's Bitcoin Mempool (https://jochen-hoenicke.de/queue/). These websites display the number and size of all unconfirmed transactions. They give a real-time view and show how the Mempool evolves. The transactions are colored by the amount of fee they pay per (virtual) byte.

Real-time view of unconfirmed transactions

Source: Screenshot by Anita Posch, https://mempool.space

Below you can see the settings in the Edge wallet. You can choose one of the ranges of the default transaction fee or a custom value.

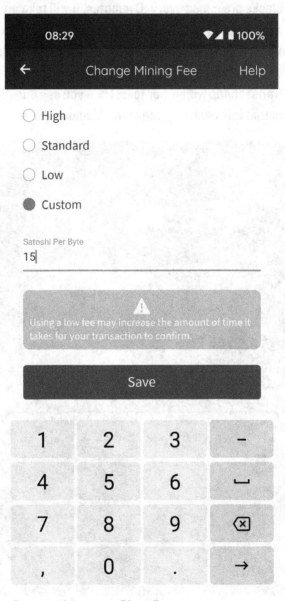

Transaction fee settings in Edge wallet

Source: Screenshot by Anita Posch, Edge wallet

Pending Transaction

Since new blocks are mined every 10 minutes, it will take an average of at least 10 minutes until your transaction is confirmed. If you set the transaction fee too low then your transaction might be pending for a longer period as the Mempool gets cleared and miners begin to re-include transactions with lower fees. Here you see one of my transactions that has been trapped in the Mempool for a month.

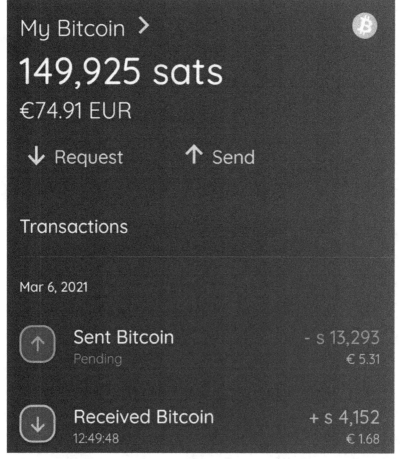

Pending transaction

Source: Screenshot by Anita Posch, Edge wallet

You can look up the status of your transaction in a Blockchain explorer (https://blockchair.com). As you can see below my transaction is 4,717 ranks away from being mined with a total of 41,610 transactions in the Mempool. I chose a fee of 5 sat per vbyte.

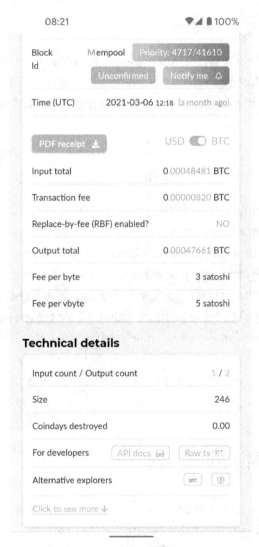

Transaction status as shown in blockexplorer

Source: Screenshot by Anita Posch, Blockchair

You do not need to follow the steps below to get your original transaction confirmed. Most low-fee transactions remain valid for days and will eventually confirm. However, there are two ways to solve the problem of the stuck transaction and get it confirmed sooner.

A Sent Transaction Is Stuck

- Replace-by-fee (RBF): some wallets allow you to set this option to yes before you send a transaction. In this case, if the original transaction gets stuck, you can set a higher fee and resend the transaction.

An Incoming Transaction Is Stuck

- Child pays for parent (CPFP): you can think of this as a parent having insufficient money for their expenses, so their child pays the difference on the parent's behalf. CPFP is a technique through which you can bump your slowly confirming incoming transactions by making a new transaction with higher fees (child transaction) using the outputs (funds) from the previous transaction (parent transaction) that is stuck.

Please look up the documentation of the wallet you are using for detailed instructions.

8.2 Buy Something With Bitcoin

Here are some directories with shops where you can spend bitcoin.
- Accepted here (https://www.acceptedhere.io)
- B2B services accepting BTC (https://cryptwerk.com/companies/b2b/btc/)

- Coinmap (https://coinmap.org/view/) physical stores accepting Bitcoin
- Spending Bitcoin (https://spending-bitcoin.com/) directory
- UseBitcoins (https://usebitcoins.info/) directory

8.3 Bitcoin Debit Cards

You can use a Bitcoin debit card to buy anything just like any other banking debit card. The difference is that it's loaded with bitcoin or altcoins. The merchants get paid in their own currency by the debit company and the charge will be deducted from your bitcoin balance, which allows you to live purely through bitcoin.

You will need to deposit your bitcoin at the debit card company, which means you give control over your coins to a third party. Deposit only as much as you need on the card and check the fees that those card companies charge.

A short list of cards that are available at the moment:
Cryptocom Visa, Binance, Bitpanda Visa, Coinbase Visa, Wirex Visa, BlockCard, Cryptopay, Nexo, Bitwala Visa, BitPay Visa, Cash App

8.4 Spending and receiving

The following are tools and services that enable you to spend and receive BTC in your daily life.
- Bity (https://bity.com/products/crypto-online-bill-pay/) pay bills online with bitcoin
- Cash App (https://cash.app/bitcoin) buy and sell BTC straight from your Cash App balance

- Strike (https://global.strike.me/) send and receive instant international payments, instant remittances and with full access to the Bitcoin network
- Piixpay (https://www.piixpay.com/?lang=en) pay anyone in EURO using your crypto
- Bitrefill (https://www.bitrefill.com/?hl=en) buy giftcards and phone refills

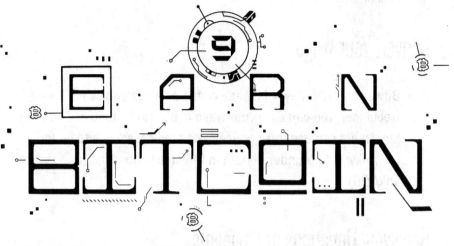

Earning Bitcoin is actually the best way to acquire it: limited or no registration, limited or no KYC identity check and no trading fees. Some of these services are only available in the US or other specific regions of the world. Since the Bitcoin space is in rapid development, this chapter can only be a lookout for what is to come.

9.1 Bitcoin Job Boards

Find a job or a client to earn Bitcoin for your work.
- BitGigs (https://bitgigs.com/)
- Coinality (https://coinality.com/)
- CanWork (https://www.canwork.io/)
- Freelance For Coins (https://freelanceforcoins.com/projects)
- Working For Bitcoin (https://workingforbitcoins.com/)

9.2 Online tasks

Earn satoshis through finishing small tasks.
- Stakwork (https://stakwork.com)
- Microlancer (https://microlancer.io/)
- Sats 4 Likes (https://kriptode.com/satsforlikes/index.html)

9.3 Convert Your Wage

- Bitwage (https://www.bitwage.com/) as an employee or freelancer, you can earn your wage in bitcoin instead of fiat. Employers can use this service to pay their team in bitcoin too. Interview with founder Jonathan Chester (https://anita. link/106).

9.4 Receiving Donations or Payments

As a nonprofit organization, a blogger or podcaster, you can easily receive tips in bitcoin/satoshis with these services:

- Tippin.me (https://tippin.me/) lets you receive lightning bitcoin tips on your website and Twitter without fees
- Tallyco.in (https://tallyco.in/) is a crowdfunding platform built on top of the Bitcoin blockchain. You can receive payments in BTC and micro-payments through Lightning at zero fees
- Lightning Gifts (https://lightning.gifts/) create fee-less bitcoin gift vouchers to share with friends & family, and your audience

9.5 Content Creators and Podcasting 2.0

With the advent of the Lightning Network, a truly groundbreaking new method of sending value and paying for content on the internet has been invented. Streaming money, a term coined by Andreas M. Antonopoulos, enables musicians, video creators and podcasters to earn money in real-time, without intermediaries. You only need a wallet that has podcasts integrated, a little bit of bitcoin and you can start listening while paying by the minute. The goal of Podcasting 2.0 and streaming money is to free content creators and the audience from ads, censorship and surveillance. Paying is voluntary, with no subscription fees and no prepayment. Be aware that at the time of writing these are all services in constant development. More about the background of podcasting 2.0 in an interview (https://anita.link/pod2) with me.

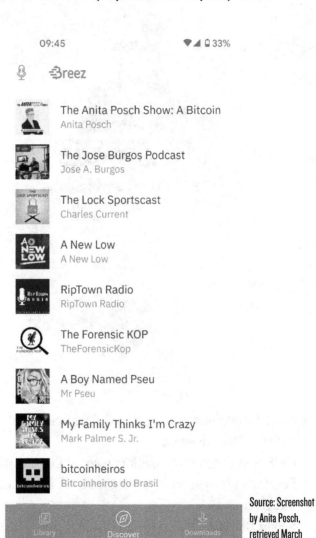

Source: Screenshot by Anita Posch, retrieved March 2021, Breez wallet

Source: Screenshot by Anita Posch, retrieved March 2021, Breez wallet

- Breez (https://breez.technology/) A non-custodial lightning wallet to listen to podcasts
- PodFriend (https://web.podfriend.com/) Podcast player
- Podstation (https://podstation.github.io/) browser extension for podcasts
- Sphinx Chat (https://sphinx.chat/) Chat and podcasting app for listeners and podcasters with their own node

- Satoshis.stream (https://satoshis.stream/) easy setup for podcasters without own node
- LN Cast (https://lncast.com/) Lightning Network podcasts, pay a small amount of satoshis and donate to listen to your favourite podcast
- LN Pay (https://lnpay.co/) Setup paywalls for your content, payable with lightning
- WordPress Lightning Paywall (https://lightning-paywall.coincharge.io/)
- Scarce.City (https://scarce.city/) Lightning auctions for Bitcoin goods and art – Interview with founder Chris Tramount (https://anita.link/91)
- Sparkshot (https://sparkshot.io/) Artists can sell their work for bitcoin

9.6 Commerce

- Breez (https://breez.technology/#business) easy to use Point-of-Sale app for merchants, restaurants, cafes... to start accepting bitcoin payments.
- BTC Pay Server (https://btcpayserver.org/) is a self-hosted, open-source cryptocurrency payment processor for e-commerce. It's secure, private, censorship-resistant and free. You can connect it to your online store, generate invoices for your accounting and earn bitcoin through lightning. With integrations for WooCommerce, Shopify, Drupal, Magento, PrestaShop, Shopware.
- Confirmo (https://confirmo.net/) accept payments with plugins for popular online stores.
- Globee (https://globee.com/) accept bitcoin with GloBee, they offer open-source plugins for all major e-commerce platforms for a commission (custodial).

- OpenNode (https://www.opennode.com/) bitcoin payments and payouts for businesses, e-commerce plugins, hosted payment pages (custodial).

9.7 Cashback and Faucets

- Fold (https://foldapp.com/) earn bitcoin on every purchase with your VISA card
- Lolli (https://www.lolli.com/) earn bitcoin when you shop at over 1,000 stores
- Pei (https://getpei.com/) link almost any debit or credit card
- Satsback (https://satsback.com/en) earn sats back from online stores
- LN Pay (https://lnpay.co/faucets/) create your own lightning faucet and pay back your audience in bitcoin.
- Purse (https://purse.io) use bitcoin to buy on Amazon and get a discount
- Satsy (https://satsy.com/) earn sats while you shop online, take surveys and play games

9.8 Gaming

- Thndr Games (https://thndr.games/games) win bitcoin prizes while playing
- Zebedee (https://zebedee.io/) with the ZEBEDEE Wallet you can play games with bitcoin, send payments inside messaging apps, collect donations on your live stream and a lot more
- Bitcoin Bounty Hunt (https://bitcoinbountyhunt.com/) a shooter game, where you can earn satoshis
- Satoshis Games (https://satoshis.games/) gaming platforms and an NFT marketplace for artists

9.9 Earn Through Investing

- SunExchange (https://thesunexchange.com/) offset your carbon footprint, buy solar cells and earn bitcoin – Interview with founder Abe Cambridge (https://anita.link/104)
- Blockstream Mining Note, STOKR (https://blockstream.com/finance/bmn/) participate in Bitcoin mining through purchasing the STOKR security token

9.10 Mining

Be aware, there are a lot of mining scams out there. Even I fell for one some years ago. That's why I never touched that possibility again. Now more legitimate businesses are launching in that space.

- Compass (https://compassmining.io/) A service that helps to buy, install and host mining hardware
- Blockstream Mining (https://blockstream.com/mining/) host your mining rigs with Blockstream's enterprise-class mining facilities and management

9.11 Lending & Borrowing

- DeFi Rate (https://defirate.com/) Overview of lending and borrowing rates

Custodial

- BlockFi (https://blockfi.com/)
- Celsius (https://celsius.network/borrow-dollars-using-crypto-as-collateral/)

- Coinloan (https://coinloan.io/)
- Coinrabbit (https://coinrabbit.io/)
- Crypto.com (https://crypto.com/earn)
- Nexo (https://nexo.io/borrow)
- SpectroCoin (https://spectrocoin.com/)

Non-Custodial

- LEND at Hodl Hodl (https://lend.hodlhodl.com/) Global P2P Bitcoin-backed non-custodial lending platform
- Sovryn (https://sovryn.app) is a non-custodial and permissionless smart contract-based system for Bitcoin lending, borrowing and margin trading.

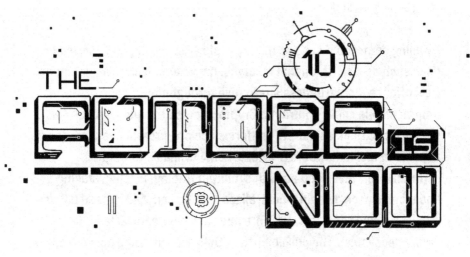

> "The future is a construction site." – ANITA POSCH

Now that you have a deeper understanding of Bitcoin and how to use it, we can dip our toes into future developments that I think will have enormous impact.

This part was co-authored by Mark Kersley with parts taken from: Andreas M. Antonopoulos' talk about Bitcoin, Layer 2 Solutions, and the Wild West of Crypto (https://youtu.be/TsbIMg-YHQk)

10.1 Decentralized Finance – DeFi

One intriguing category of new applications is called decentralized finance, or DeFi. Decentralized finance aims to expand upon the monetary freedom offered and inspired by Bitcoin, and introduce these features to the whole crypto ecosystem. It's all well and good owning bitcoin or other decentralized assets, but when most people go to buy, sell or even hold their assets long-term, they use a centralized entity such as an exchange.

By using centralized entities these people are exposing themselves to risks such as KYC, fractional reserves, hacks and insider manipulation. DeFi offers a more trustless alternative through the use of programmable smart contracts. Crypto-assets are digital and, as such, they are programmable. DeFi platforms use pre-programmed contracts to perform tasks that were previously only available through centralized entities such as swaps, margin trading, lending, staking and more. By removing the centralized 'middlemen' and instead using publicly visible contracts, DeFi provides a fairer financial layer to the crypto ecosystem. The possibilities of DeFi are still being discovered and built. One day, the entire global financial system may be decentralized.

Most DeFi applications are developed and run on the Ethereum (ETH) network – the second largest crypto-asset by market cap at the time of writing. Ethereum is very developer friendly and focuses on smart contract development through languages like Solidity. Therefore, it has been the perfect incubation ground for DeFi platforms in recent years. Popular use cases for DeFi on Ethereum are decentralized exchanges (DEXs), lending platforms and pegged stable-coins like USDT.

DeFi platforms can utilise tokens from other chains through a process called wrapping. This involves sending an asset from another blockchain to a smart contract peg. Let's use 1 bitcoin as an example. This peg will hold (lock up) the bitcoin sent to it and mint the equivalent version of that bitcoin on the Ethereum network. Examples of this are wrapped bitcoin (WBTC) and Ren bitcoin (renBTC). These pegged tokens can be used on the DeFi application in place of the original asset and because the smart contract holds the original asset, there can be no issue of a 'double-spend'. When a user wishes to withdraw their assets back to their native chain, the smart contract will burn the token it minted and send the user their original asset on the native chain. This process enables DeFi to work for virtually any digital token.

Bitcoin's development is slower and has a more conservative approach than many other blockchains like Ethereum. This for a good reason: security. But developers in the Bitcoin space haven't been sleeping – aside from the Lightning Network a lot of Bitcoin-native platforms and applications have been developed.

10.1.1 Bitcoin-Native Protocols and Platforms

10.1.1.1 Rootstock

Rootstock (RSK) is a network that looks to bring smart contract capabilities to Bitcoin. It is merge-mined with Bitcoin, meaning between 40 and 75% of Bitcoin miners actually process the transactions of the RSK network. This means that RSK is secured by more hash power that any other blockchain in the world, excluding Bitcoin of course. Similarly to Ethereum solutions, RSK uses the wrapping process to introduce bitcoin to the network. However, since the network itself is merge-mined by Bitcoin miners it can be considered the most secure and trustless network to build DeFi on currently. It has the most appeal to Bitcoiners and those who long for DeFi solutions for Bitcoin, but do not wish to lose the decentralization, trustlessness and security offered by the Bitcoin network.

Rootstock has been in development since 2014 and launched it's mainnet in 2018. The RSK network has fast block times, processing each block in 15-30 seconds. Applications can be built on top of RSK using similar techniques as Ethereum such as with the Solidity development language. The gas costs for RSK are significantly less

than that of Ethereum; at the time of writing, Ethereum transactions cost an average of $60 whilst RSK transactions cost an average of $0.50. Due to it's speed and customisation potential, rollups can be introduced to applications built on Rootstock to further decrease transaction speed and costs, potentially as low as less than $0.01 per transaction.

10.1.1.2 Sovryn

Sovryn is an example of one such platform being built on the Rootstock network. Sovryn is creating a DeFi platform for bitcoin as well as many other assets via bridges to other chains including Ethereum and Binance Smart Chain (BSC). It is a non-custodial and permissionless contract-based system primarily used for bitcoin lending, borrowing and margin trading. There is no KYC for Sovryn and it never demands custody of your funds, not your keys, not your coins! It currently features a low-cost spot exchange, margin trading, lending/borrowing, liquidity providing/mining and some non-fungible token (NFT) functionality. It uses a fastBTC relay to quickly convert bitcoin to Rootstock smart bitcoin (rBTC) for use on Sovryn. Future developments will bring multiple assets from multiple chains to Sovryn, as well as an NFT marketplace, token launchpad, perpetual swaps and overcollateralized bitcoin-backed stable-coins. The vision of Sovryn is not to be just another DeFi platform, but the financial operating system of the world.

Sovryn is not a company or centralized entity. It consists of many contributors whose goal is to create the trustless monetary layer that ideally should have been created on top of Bitcoin long ago. Sovryn ensures decentralized governance of the protocol via a form of democratic system called the Bitocracy, an evolved version of a vetocracy. This involves the staking of SOV tokens in return for voting power and fee rewards. All protocol level decisions must pass voting in the Bitocracy to be implemented. The staking mechanism ensures that voters are incentivized to provide educated votes in favor of proposals that would benefit the Sovryn ecosystem and against harmful proposals. At the time of writing, Sovryn has just begun its token trading and are looking to release multiple bridges and new features. It will be interesting to watch the project develop.

I interviewed founder Edan Yago, where he explores most of these topics – listen at https://anita.link/l05

10.1.1.3 Thorchain

Similar to Sovryn, Thorchain was founded upon the realization that centralized means of transferring ownership of cryptoassets are fundamentally flawed. Born in 2018, Thorchain was created to serve as a replacement to centralized exchanges (CEX), and instead facilitates cross-chain decentralized crypto exchange (DEX). Thorchain connects between different chains through its own cross-chain bridge, thematically named the Bifröst Protocol. The Bifröst allows native token swaps across different chains, meaning there is no need for synthetic or wrapped versions of tokens. Crucially, Thorchain is non-custodial and is 100% decentralized.

Thorchain operates mostly the same as other DEXs such as Sovryn; it utilizes an automated market maker model (AMM) to process and maintain exchanges. However, Thorchain does not run on another blockchain, like Sovryn runs on RSK for example. Thorchain is instead its own independent blockchain that was built using the Cosmos SDK. This has allowed Thorchain to force its own RUNE token as the base swap asset, meaning that every swap pair is a RUNE-x pair. Therefore users are able to swap, for example, BTC for ETH through the RUNE

token's intermediary role. This would in fact function as a swap of BTC to RUNE, then a swap of RUNE to ETH. This has allowed the RUNE token's utility to command value: RUNE can be used to provide liquidity to the AMM pools in return for a share of fees and can be traded and speculated upon via the open market.

10.1.1.4 Babelfish Money

Within crypto, there are many pegged tokens which are widely referred to as 'stablecoins'. These are very popular and are commonly used to store, transfer and use wealth with minimal short-term volatility. There are many stablecoins pegged to the US Dollar such as Tether (USDT), US Dollar Coin (USDC), Binance USD (BUSD) and DAI, all of which are designed to maintain a value of $1.00 per token. Whilst these stablecoins form a very useful element of the crypto ecosystem, having different stablecoins on different networks has resulted in barriers to fluid liquidity across platforms.

Named after the translation device in Douglas Adams' 'The Hitchhiker's Guide to the Galaxy', Babelfish aims to act as a cross-chain aggregator for all stablecoins. The vision is that anyone will be able to use Babelfish to convert any stablecoin to another, all backed by Bitcoin.

The process will follow the same steps as classical fiat-stablecoin token issuance: a user will send one type of stablecoin and the protocol will mint convertible stablecoins (XUSD) to the user. The protocol invests the original stablecoins across DeFi platforms to earn a yield, which will then fund governance and a bitcoin layer 2 insurance pool; the yield will be re-invested weekly into a community-owned pool of bitcoin – the ultimate asset for insurance.

The governance of the protocol is community controlled. Every time somebody uses the protocol and receives minted XUSD, they also receive FISH tokens. FISH is the governance token upon which voting power is attributed. Therefore, users can vote in the direction of the protocol using these FISH tokens.

Babelfish will be launching its initial token sale on Sovryn's Origin platform – a decentralized launchpad governed by the Sovryn Bitocracy.

10.1.1.5 Money on Chain

Money on Chain (MoC) is a DeFi protocol that holds four significant tokens within it. The idea is to provide more options to Bitcoiners, to improve upon their bitcoin performance and use cases whilst allowing them full control of their private keys. Money on Chain also operates on the RSK network, maintaining its Bitcoin focus.

The first token MoC offers is Dollar on Chain (DoC). This is the first 100% bitcoin-collateralized token, pegged 1:1 to the US dollar.

Next is BPRO, a token that returns passive income through distributed sharing of pooled profits and other means. BPRO holders can benefit from free long leverage, courtesy of DoC token holders. BPRO holders also earn from liquidity mining and a share of fees generated by the MoC protocol. Essentially, holding BPRO is like holding bitcoin, at a slight leveraged long, whilst earning passive income from your bitcoin.

The third token offered by MoC is a BTC/USD instrument named BTCx. BTCx is essentially a tokenized representation of a bitcoin leveraged long position. These tokens are minted when a user sends BTC to the

smart contract and come at a variable interest rate cost (which is fixed upon contract creation). The interest payments go to ฿ PRO holders.

Lastly, the MoC protocol also includes a governance token, conveniently named the Money on Chain token (MOC). This allows MOC holders to stake in return for voting/veto power and staking rewards, both from fees paid in the platform and liquidity mining. Users are entitled to a discount on platform fees when they pay using the MOC token.

To conclude, Money on Chain is a self-contained Bitcoin ecosystem, on RSK, which looks to provide multiple decentralized and non-custodial use cases specifically for Bitcoiners.

10.1.1.6 Liquid Network

The Liquid Network is a federated sidechain-based settlement network for individuals and exchanges, enabling faster, more confidential Bitcoin transactions and the issuance of digital assets. It's a separate blockchain that extends the functionalities of bitcoin with layered technologies. Liquid does not use proof-of-work, blocks are signed on a per minute base by 15 functionaries. It enhances privacy through confidential transactions and assets, where the amount and type of the asset that is being sent is hidden, while it is still cryptographically guaranteed that no more coins can be spent than are available.

There are a variety of use cases for Liquid:

- fast transactions between exchanges
- individuals can use L-BTC through the Blockstream Green, Aqua, Elements, or Sideswap wallets
- Peer-to-Peer exchange HodlHodl uses L-BTC for its lending service

- the decentralized exchange Bisq will integrate L-BTC as its base layer
- anyone can issue new assets, including stablecoins like Tether USDt (already supported by Liquid) and security tokens, which can be traded freely within the network

Liquid shows that you can do anything with Bitcoin. You don't need a new blockchain or a new token. The native currency of Liquid is L-BTC, where you lock in your bitcoin and get the same amount of L-BTC for it. Therefore there will be only 21 million L-BTC ever. Liquid transactions are cheaper, faster and more private than bitcoin transactions. Although it's a federated sidechain transactions cannot be censored. The functionaries are black boxes, which can only be turned off by the operators. The trade-off is that Bitcoin peg-out transactions must be done through a Liquid member.

10.1.1.7 RGB

RGB is a smart contract system, working on Layer 2 and 3 on top of Bitcoin and the Lightning Network. It is designed with confidentiality and scalability in mind.

Possible use cases are:
- Issue digital fungible assets, like stock, bonds and other forms of securities
- Create different forms of collectibles (non-fungible assets)
- Create and manage sovereign/decentralized identities
- Design and run other forms of arbitrary-complex smart contracts

By their abilities RGB smart contracts go beyond what is possible with Ethereum-like smart contract systems, providing more layered,

scalable, private and safe approach, where the ownership of the smart contract state is separated from the smart contract creation.

10.2 NFTs

The other category that I think is extremely interesting is NFTs, or non-fungible tokens. These are tokens that, instead of representing units of currency, represent unique objects, items, or properties in the form that is distinguishable from one another and are therefore non-fungible. So let's think of an art piece that is represented by a deeds document. That document could be a digital token that can be traded like bitcoin, or the deed to your house, or your car, or any other physical item or specific piece of land. It's basically taking things that exist in the real world or taking digital intellectual property – like a song or a brand – and tokenizing it so that it becomes something that can be digitally traded. We haven't even scratched the surface in that domain so far.

The first NFT platform on top of Bitcoin was Counterparty, founded even before Ethereum in 2014. In recent months more Bitcoin based NFT platforms are popping up. Raretoshi, and Azool.art are NFT platforms based on the Liquid Network. On Watafan trading cards that have collective value are backed by Rootstock smart contracts. Sovryn and RGB are developing NFT platforms by the time of writing this book.

10.3 Governance

Finally, the third category that excites me for the future is the opportunity of applying this to the areas of identity and human governance. The ability to have tokenized human identities, where you do not have to reveal who you are but can choose to reveal various aspects at a time. I can prove that I have a degree from a University using a non-fungible token without telling you my name. I can prove that I am licensed to drive without giving you my entire history. I can prove that I am creditworthy, or trustworthy, vaccinated or whatever other characteristic you can think of. These various tokens that you can assign to individuals allow you to be in control of these things, no need for a government or a corporation like Facebook to do that. Then you can take those tokens and use them for governance purposes. The ability to vote in my homeowner's association, in my parent-teacher association, in my municipality, and all the way up into voting at the United Nations as one of 7 and 1/2 billion citizens of this planet with a digital voting token. Radical change towards direct democracy is possible with these technologies.

These are things we're talking about 10, 15, 20, 25 years into the future. But if you understand how this technology works, and you see the seeds we're planting today, you can see these as natural developments that come out of this technology.

Glossary

Cantillon Effect

French economist Richard Cantillon suggested that inflation occurs gradually and that the new supply of money has a localized effect on inflation, effectively originating the concept of non-neutral money. Furthermore, he posited that the original recipients of new money enjoy higher standards of living at the expense of later recipients.[1]

Central bank

A central bank, reserve bank, or monetary authority is an institution that manages the currency and monetary policy of a state or formal monetary union, and oversees their commercial banking system.[2]

Currency

A currency is a system of money in common use defined by governments. Many jurisdictions define their national currency as legal tender, it is money declared by law to be valid for the payment of debts and can't be refused as payment.

---

1 Cantillon Effect on Wikipedia, https://en.wikipedia.org/wiki/Richard_Cantillon
2 Central bank on Wikipedia, https://en.wikipedia.org/wiki/Central_bank

Fiat money

A currency (a medium of exchange) established as money, often by government regulation. Fiat money does not have intrinsic value and does not have use value (inherent utility, such as a cow or beaver pelt might have). It has value only because a government maintains its value, or because parties engaging in exchange agree on its value.[3]

All nation state currencies are fiat currencies. Since 1971 fiat currencies are not backed by gold. The word "fiat" is Latin and means "let it be done".

Fractional-reserve banking

Fractional-reserve banking, practiced by commercial banks worldwide, involves banks accepting deposits from customers and making loans to borrowers while holding in reserve an amount equal to only a fraction of the bank's deposit liabilities. Bank reserves are held as cash in the bank or as balances in the bank's account at a central bank. The country's central bank determines the minimum amount that banks must hold in liquid assets, called the "reserve requirement" or "reserve ratio". This rate varies from country to country. In March 2020 the FED abolished this minimum reserve requirement due to the pandemic. Canada, the UK, New Zealand, Australia, Sweden and Hong Kong have no reserve requirements.

Full node

A full node is a software program that fully validates transactions and blocks. You can run a full node on your home computer or on a

---

3 Fiat money on Wikipedia, https://en.wikipedia.org/wiki/Fiat_money

Rasperry Pi. Almost all full nodes help the network by accepting transactions and blocks from other full nodes, validating those transactions and blocks, and then relaying them to further full nodes. They are a part of the peer-to-peer network.

Hasher

A specialized computer device, called ASIC that is only used for Bitcoin mining.

International Monetary Fund

The IMF is an international financial institution, headquartered in Washington, D.C., consisting of 190 countries working to foster global monetary cooperation, secure financial stability, facilitate international trade, promote high employment and sustainable economic growth, and reduce poverty around the world while periodically depending on the World Bank for its resources. Formed in July 1944, at the Bretton Woods Conference primarily by the ideas of Harry Dexter White and John Maynard Keynes, it came into formal existence in 1945 with 29 member countries and the goal of reconstructing the international monetary system. It now plays a central role in the management of balance of payments difficulties and international financial crises. Countries contribute funds to a pool through a quota system from which countries experiencing balance of payments problems can borrow money.[4]

Lender of last resort

A lender of last resort (LOLR) is the institution in a financial system that acts as the provider of liquidity to a financial institution which finds

---

4 IMF on Wikipedia, https://en.wikipedia.org/wiki/International_Monetary_Fund

itself unable to obtain sufficient liquidity in the inter-bank lending market and other facilities or sources have been exhausted. It is, in effect, a government guarantee of liquidity to financial institutions.[5]

M0 Monetary Base

The monetary base (M0) is the total amount of a currency in physical paper and coin that is either in circulation in the hands of the public or in the form of commercial bank deposits held in the central bank's reserves.[6]

M1 Money Stock

M1 is a narrow measure of the money supply that includes physical currency, demand deposits, traveler's checks, and other checkable deposits. M1 does not include financial assets, such as savings accounts and bonds.[7]

M2 Money Stock

M2 is a measure of the money supply that includes cash, checking deposits, and easily convertible near money as savings deposits, money market securities and mutual funds. These assets are less liquid than M1 and not as suitable as exchange mediums, but they can be quickly converted into cash or checking deposits. M2 is closely watched as an indicator of money supply and future inflation, and as a target of central bank monetary policy.[8]

---

5 Lender of last resort on Wikipedia, https://en.wikipedia.org/wiki/Lender_of_last_resort
6 Monetary Base, https://www.investopedia.com/terms/m/monetarybase.asp
7 M1 Money, https://www.investopedia.com/terms/m/m1.asp
8 M2 Money, https://www.investopedia.com/terms/m/m2.asp

Panopticon

The panopticon is a type of institutional building and a system of control designed by the English philosopher and social theorist Jeremy Bentham in the 18th century. The concept of the design is to allow all prisoners of an institution to be observed by a single security guard, without the inmates being able to tell whether they are being watched.[9]

Peer-to-Peer Network

A system of equally privileged, equipotent participants without a hierarchy on the network. The Bitcoin peer-to-peer network is a decentralized system of computers running the Bitcoin software that is validating and distributing transactions.

Rehypothecation

The action of a broker who pledges with a bank or other lender securities already left on deposit with him by a customer as a pledge for their purchase on margin.

Seed

12-24 words that secure your funds on the blockchain. Anyone with the seed has control over the funds on the associated addresses.

Surveillance capitalism

A term coined by Shoshana Zuboff. It describes the systematic commodification of personal data by centralized monopolistic companies with the core purpose of profit-making.

---

9 Panopticon on Wikipedia, https://en.wikipedia.org/wiki/Panopticon

Wallet

Software or hardware that holds all your bitcoin addresses and private keys. Use it to send, receive, and store your bitcoin.

Credits

Special thanks to Sovryn for contributing to the creation of this book (editing, typesetting, design, translations).

I would also like to thank the following people for lending their time and expertise:

Exiledsurfer, Jameson Lopp, Nic Carter, Andreas M. Antonopoulos, Caitlin Long, Maya Zehavi, Lyn Alden, Alena Vranova, Thomas Voegtlin, Max Hillebrand, Hass McCook, Ryan Gentry, embarrassedOK, Erik24020105, Chris Chester, Johannes Grill, Daniel Pichler, Stephanie Jagl-Posch.

Disclaimer

The contents of this book do not constitute financial, tax or legal advice, but are for informational purposes only. The information is intended to inform a set of best practices. It may not address risks specific to your situation, and if it does not, you should modify appropriately. While this information may inform best practices, there is no guarantee that following this advice will sufficiently ensure the security of your digital assets. In addition, this information is only a window on best practices at a specific moment in time. Be aware that the Bitcoin & blockchain ecosystems may have evolved and the risk assessments of specific products may have changed since the publication of this book. In other words: be cautious, be careful, and be aware of the current Bitcoin & blockchain landscape before you use this information.

Author

Anita Posch is a Bitcoin advocate, author, solopreneur and host of the Anita Posch show. She is a member of the board of Bitcoin Austria – an educational non-profit organization.

Anita's goal is to bring Bitcoin to billions through her educational work. She has developed a Bitcoin podcast, a YouTube channel and wrote the book (L)earn Bitcoin. She has also interviewed people from all around the world including some from developing countries like Nigeria, South Africa, Venezuela, and Afghanistan about the effects of Bitcoin on people's freedom.

In early 2020 she was the first Bitcoiner to visit Zimbabwe to research the country's monetary situation as well as the adoption rate of Bitcoin and to report on the results in her podcast. The goal was, through interviews, to build a bridge between people who live under flawed democracies or authoritarian regimes to the rest of the world and to show how Bitcoin could improve their living conditions and financial freedom.

Bitcoin is money from the people, for the people. Its mathematical rules can't be corrupted – neither by governments nor by billionaires. This guarantees a level of fairness that cannot be achieved in traditional human-driven systems. It gives underprivileged individuals, such as people from developing nations, women, and oppressed minority groups, the chance to participate globally in a free and private manner

with each other. This freedom to exchange value, unleashing people's creativity and innovation, is what drives Anita Posch.

> "Bitcoin might be our only tool to secure the human right to privacy and freedom of transaction. It's a medium of liberation for billions of people and a defence mechanism for privacy in our ever more digital lives." – ANITA POSCH

Before she started her educational Bitcoin work in 2017, Anita gained over 20 years of experience in web development, e-commerce, and online business. Disillusioned by the centralized nature of the internet, consumerism and surveillance capitalism she spent 2016 in Berlin on a mission to make a change.

In early 2017 she attended a talk about Bitcoin and open blockchain technology and the positive impact it could have on society. She realized that a technology that is permissionless, inflation-proof and a global internet money could free billions of people, disenfranchised by current financial power dynamics. Bitcoin is unstoppable money that can be used by anyone regardless of who they are. It's neutral, not controlled by any company or government, while at the same time being an internet protocol, financial rails that are built for a common good.

Anita translated two volumes of The Internet of Money (https://anita. link/idg2) by Andreas M. Antonopoulos into German. Her research and activities around Bitcoin are discussed in media all over the world: Bitcoin Magazine, CoinDesk, What Bitcoin Did, Bayern2, Deutschlandfunk, Radio FM4, and ARD television, among others.

Anita Posch regularly tweets on https://twitter.com/anitaposch.